1.65

An Irish Saint

An Irish Saint

The Life Story of Ann Preston
known also as "Holy Ann"

❍ ❍ ❍

By HELEN E. BINGHAM

With an Introduction by
REV. E. L. SIMMONDS, B.D., M.A.
Principal of Toronto Bible College

TWENTY-NINTH EDITION

———◆———

PRINTED BY
MALLOY LITHOGRAPHING, INC.,
ANN ARBOR, MICHIGAN

CONTENTS

Introduction

It was in the winter of 1930 that this book, "An Irish Saint" came into the hands of a young man who, like Ann, had come to Canada from the Old Country.

He was amazed and deeply moved at what he read. He had always gone to church and said his prayers but he had never expected that the latter would be answered in any particular way. Here, however, was an ignorant Irish woman who could neither read nor write, but who *did* receive answers to her prayers. And what answers they were!

Ann prayed, not just in vague generalities, but for definite, specific things. It was possible, therefore, to tell beyond the shadow of a doubt whether the prayers were answered or not.

Once Ann was challenged to pray that water would be found in an entirely dry well, and by the next morning there was water in that well, and it stayed there, the well did not go dry again. On another occasion, when she was unable to walk because of an ankle injury, her doctor prescribed a fresh egg every day. Eggs were impossible to obtain, but for three weeks a hen came to Ann's house each day and provided the fresh egg.

This book carries the record of not just one, nor a dozen, nor a hundred, but of a lifetime of such answered prayers.

The young man wondered why God should not answer *his* prayers as He did those of Ann. Closer reading of the book showed that answers to prayer were merely one aspect of Ann's living relationship with God, a relationship that began through a personal acceptance of Christ as Saviour. Ann knew the Lord as a constantly present Friend and she not only talked with Him as one would with any human companion but she also heard His voice in an intimate and amazing way.

It was this close fellowship with God, and the incontrovertible proof that it gave of His reality and His accessibility to those who believe in Christ, that were largely responsible for the conversion of the young man who read the book.

Today he is happy, after over thirty years of knowing Ann's God, to write this Introduction, and to add his prayer that God will continue to use this brief story of Ann's life to the blessing of many another reader and to the glory of His own great name.

E. L. SIMMONDS.

(Rev. E. L. Simmonds, B.D., M.A., is Principal of Toronto Bible College)—*Publisher's Note.*

Preface

THE BELIEF that the life that brought such blessing to the home of my girlhood would, by its fragrance, minister acceptably to the wider household of faith, is the motive that has prompted the writing of this biography.

Then the persistent requests from the wide circle of friends, who felt that the marvellous grace manifested in this life under review was worthy of some record in the annals of the Church, have urged me on in the pleasant task.

The work was conceived before the death of the subject, and the greater portion of this story was taken down directly from the lips now silent. Many times before had she been approached for a sketch of her life, but only in the last two years did she feel that her Father would be glorified in its publication. Abler writers might have been selected for the purpose, but they would have lacked the long acquaintance which was essential to the right setting of this broken narrative.

The years .that Ann Preston spent beneath our roof furnished frequent occasions to hear the stories herein recorded, told and re-told, with daily supplements being wrought out in actual experiences before our eyes.

Thrown, when nearing her ninetieth year, into the midst of a household of seven rollicking boys and girls, ranging from the early school days to maturity, it afforded an excellent opportunity of watching this unique character at well-nigh every angle of observation.

The strenuous activity of our country life furnished little occasion for the maintenance of her influence by the arts of the recluse. But then her saintliness never bore the odor of the nunnery. Those who associate holiness with the seclusion of the cloister will be disappointed here.

At her advanced age Ann had lost none of the zest of life, but entered into the household affairs, took an equal interest in the labours of the men, and. was a delightful companion to our big baby brother.

The mind that has only conceived sanctity under a clerical garb and sustained by ministerial dignity should find a refreshing tonic here.

Sufficient for such to see this woman, to whom heaven seemed always open and her well-nigh

10

every petition granted, rambling in the bush with my youngest brother; or in the winter time when the snow was deep being coaxed to go with him for just one ride down the little hill at the back of the house. Take one look at the old saint of ninety lying flat on the hand-sleigh, being piloted by my little brother down the hill; perchance a hidden knoll unexpectedly precipitating a roll in the soft snow; let that hearty Irish laugh dispel any fears you may have, and when it is all over and you listen to that half apology that "the boy had to have something to amuse him", scarcely veiling her own pleasure in the escapade, and you will conclude that you must save your robes of purple and your garments of white for other occasions, and come to this book with the idea of studying religion in homespun.

The best testimony to the quality of that life was the fact that Ann never entered a home without leaving a benediction, and that in those where she stayed the longest will be found the greatest confidence in her saintliness.

While among the wider circle of readers into whose hands this sketch may fall there may be those who will be tempted to doubt some of the

11

striking evidences of the power of God in this life, the thousands who knew her will have no question as to the veracity of any story that came forth from her lips.

No claim being made to literary ability, no apology is necessary for its absence.

The indispensable assistance of the most intimate friends of the departed, especially of Mrs. F. Hughes, of Toronto, and the constant help and encouragement of my dear husband, enable me to send forth this little tribute of love to the memory of the now truly sainted Ann.—*H. E. B.*

1

A FOREVIEW

SHE WAS IRISH, and a saint. The terms may to some minds seem incongruous and may not generally be associated. Hot Celtic blood may possibly not be easily turned into the channel of sanctity, but nevertheless Ireland has had its saints, and Ann Preston was one of them. She might not be able to claim lineal descent from St. Patrick, and to be sure saintliness does not always descend a family tree. But then she was connected with the same source of life for "He that sanctifieth and they that are sanctified are all of one".

She was Irish, anyway; there could be no doubt about that. Although she had not trodden the green sod of the Old Land for well-nigh seventy years, her face had not lost anything of the national characteristic, and to hear her speak but a few sentences would have settled that question beyond the suspicion of a doubt.

And then she was a saint; at least so everybody said that had ever known her, and she was known to thousands, and her influence felt far beyond the limits of any common life. There was surely something remarkable in the career of a poor woman, when at its close ministers of all denominations gathered around the casket bearing the lifeless remains, and one of our large city churches was packed to the doors to listen to the testimony of those representing all branches of the Church, as they bore witness that the life of this sainted woman had been an untold blessing to them. There would have been nothing strange about this had the coffin contained the remains of one of earth's great ones. Culture or wealth has an attractive power, but this woman was unlettered and illiterate. She had no wealth to bequeath and not a living relative to mourn her loss. She had lived during the last years like Elijah, as the guest of a poor widow, who ministered to her needs. Her very coffin was a gift of love, and her dust was deposited in the lot of another.

On the following Sunday the Mayor of Toronto testified in his church, "I have had two honours this week. It has been my privilege to have an interview with the President of the United States. This is a great honour. Then I have been pall-bearer to Holy Ann," and no reflection was cast upon the head of the great Republic when he added, "of the two honours I prize the latter most."

A life with such an influence is surely worthy of some memorial, and it has been our endeavour to so set forth the authentic records that she, being dead, may yet speak, and that the testimony which she bore may continue to bless the lives of those who read it. We would fain hope that the story may prove an antidote for the materialism and unbelief of our day, as the facts recorded bear emphatic testimony to the inerrancy of the Word of God and furnish abundant evidence that behind that Word God still lives to make its every promise sure. On no other ground shall we find the explanation of the mysteries wrapped up in the life of our Irish saint.

2

EARLY HOME LIFE

"We were by nature children of wrath, even as the rest."
—Eph. 2:3.

THAT SAINTSHIP did not come by natural genera-
tion in the case of Ann Preston is very evident
from the fact that at the time of her birth neither
her father nor mother made any pretension to piety.
In fact, it would seem that they had little to do
with religious things in any shape or form. Her
home was one of those typical Irish shanties in
the secluded village of Ballamacally, just about a
mile from the little town of Markethill, in the
County of Armagh.

We do not care to paint the house any prettier
than it really was, or to dress it in any way with
poetic fancy. The thatched roof was just as sombre
as that of any other cottage, and the usual stack
of peat did not enhance the beauty of the landscape.
Moreover, the pig-pen was in just as close proximity
to the back door as custom and convenience permitted an Irishman to have it. In those days there
were no haunting dreams of germs and microbes,
and the grunt and squeal were not out of harmony

with the usual music of the household. James Preston was a hard-working man; at least he laboured for long hours in his occupation as a herdsman. Then after the day's toil it was necessary for him to spend the evening hours tilling the little potato patch attached to his cottage. Even the women had to take their share of this kind of work in order to keep hunger away from the door.

Ann was fortunate in having two older sisters to sing her lullabies; but to compensate for this bit of good fortune, after nursing two sisters and a solitary boy that made their appearance later, Ann was hired to rock the cradle in a neighbor's home.

When asked for her childhood reminiscences two things seemed to have left their imprint, one upon the mind, and the other may have made more impression in other ways at the time, for she quaintly concluded her story by adding, "I mind that for the whipping I got."

It is natural that the entrance of death into any home should leave an indelible mark upon the child mind, and Ann recalled the dissolution of a godly aunt who was sent to bless them for a short time. Beneath that roof she had witnessed a good confession, and in that closing scene it was manifest

17

that "Blessed are the dead that die in the Lord."
Ann was too young to think much of eternal things
then, but her older sister Mary dated the beginning
of a new life to that Providence that brought the
influence of this aunt to their home.

The other memory of childhood—that is, of the
very early days—took her back over ninety years.
Wholesome chastening should leave a long impression. Pity the child whose waywardness is not
marked by the memory of some rebuke or correc-
tion. When not more than five years of age Ann's
mother took her down by the little stream that
meandered near by the village, and left her in
charge of some cotton which she was bleaching on
the banks. Her instructions were very clear. On
no account was she to leave the spot or lose sight of
the goods. Even amid the honesty of old Ireland
some caution was necessary.

But Ann was a real child of Eve, and the forbid-
den thing became the attractive thing. Her tempter
came in the shape of a young girl, who just wanted
Ann to run across the fields to her house to get
something for her. This seeming friend would not
take Ann's refusal, but prevailed by promising
watchful care of the cotton in her absence. Ann

sped across the intervening space as fast as her legs would carry her, but when she returned from her errand she found that girl and cotton were both missing, and she was left alone to the flogging that followed.

Ann's school education began and ended in little more than a week, for in that time she exhausted the patience of the teacher to the point of despair, and finally, after many vain attempts to teach her the first letters of the alphabet, he gave her a significant tap upon the head as he pathetically remarked before the class, "Poor Ann! She can never learn anything." And with this she was sent home in disgrace. Whether her case was absolutely hopeless we do not know, but her education terminated in this abrupt way.

However, if her mind was vacant, her bones were not lazy, and she enjoyed little respite from work. In the family with which she was at once hired, the father herded cattle for a living. On Sunday, in order to allow him to carry on his devotions, the hired girl was deputed to herd the cattle, and Ann's week of toil was followed by a long day in the fields, where, in order to fight off the tremendous temptation to sleep at her task, she used to occupy herself in piecing quilts. This, of course, did not help her

19

into a life of saintship. Compulsory Sabbath-breaking was not a very good beginning.

But this was only the commencement of evils. Her master kept a number of servants, and they were not of the immaculate type. The absence of master and mistress was usually the signal for an evening's fun and frolic, and their festivities were considered incomplete without a good supply of Irish whiskey. For some reason Ann had a horror of fire-water. She may have seen some of its brutalizing effects in her home surroundings, but, however that may be, she persistently refused to drink with the other hired help on these occasions.

Whether sunken into that terrible condition of depravity which takes delight in seeing others indulge in evil, or whether simply stung by the reproof of her refusal, they determined to force her to take part with them. By sheer strength some held her down while the others poured the liquor down her throat, and then with diabolical delight they made sport of her as she sat helplessly appealing to them to put her to bed, mumbling over and over again in her intoxicated state, "Fitter I was saying my prayers than sitting here drunk."

It was a miracle that she did not early become a drunkard, for after this first taste she used to hunt for the hidden whiskey bottle of her master while minding the cattle on Sunday. But while thus stealing an occasional drink, she still dreaded the tavern. Occasionally her master would drive some seven miles to cut turf, and after the hard day's work he would take the servants into the tavern to treat them on the homeward journey. On these occasions Ann always refused to go in, and would often run to her home through the dark, although she was so nervous that she would afterward coax her father to accompany her back to her place because of the superstitious dread of the will-o'-the-wisp.

Just about this time a well-meaning effort was made to impart to her some religious instruction, but it failed as ignominiously as the attempt to teach her letters. A good Methodist sister undertook to teach her the Lord's Prayer, but was shocked at the revelation of ignorance when she commenced. She said to Ann, "Now, repeat it after me, 'Our Father which art in heaven,'" and Ann at once followed in parrot-like fashion, 'Now, repeat it after me, Our Father which art in heaven." But when constant repetition failed to make the least impression on the memory, this good friend finally abandoned the task in despair.

3

THE GREAT CHANGE

"Except ye turn, and become as little children, ye shall in no wise enter into the kingdom of heaven."
—Matt. 18:3 (R.V.).

FOR FOUR YEARS Ann continued in this situation, and then seemed to fall into worse surroundings, for after six months in her next home she was actually contemplating taking a situation with the low saloonkeeper of the place. God very graciously arrested her downward steps, and providentially opened a situation for her with a Christian mistress. Mrs. McKay hated liquor, for her husband had been driven to the asylum through it, and while he was at this time at home once more, yet her strong dislike to the intoxicating cup was often expressed, and Ann was certainly fully warned along this line. Mrs. McKay's goodness was not merely that of the negative kind, for she had positive piety of the warm Irish Methodist type and she sought to influence all who came beneath her roof. She observed family prayer, and Ann was invited to join them in worship. It was a new epoch in her experience, although her dull mind comprehended very little of what was being said. Her ignorance of religious matters may be judged from the fact that when asked to bring the New Testament she went and brought a newspaper. The book had never been used in any home that Ann had ever lived in, so that her ignorance was but natural.

Mrs. McKay was very anxious to win her hired help, but she acted quite judiciously in that for some time she omitted to press Ann to accompany her to religious meetings. She finally ventured to invite her to come to class meeting. After a little pressure, Ann agreed to go. It was all so new to her that she looked on in open-mouthed wonder as she saw some weeping and others praising God. As things proceeded she seemed to be somewhat disgusted. To her it seemed like religious cant. She even watched to see whether the crying was real, or whether they were wetting their faces with their fingers. She hardly knew what to think of the whole matter.

After dinner that day the mistress rang the bell and Ann entered the parlor, and was surprised when she was invited to sit down. Mrs. McKay opened the conversation with, "Well, Ann, how did you like class meeting?"

Ann's answer was a non-committal "I don't know", although if she had spoken her mind she would have called them a lot of hypocrites.

"Well," said Mrs. McKay, "won't you go again?"

Ann doggedly replied, "I don't think so."

When pressed for a reason, she stated that she had nothing to say in the meeting anyway. She felt utterly out of place when others were speaking and praying and weeping, while she sat as stolid as a post. In order to help her, Mrs. McKay suggested that she had some reasons to praise God, saying, "Who gives you food to eat and raiment to wear?" This well-meaning question missed the mark in Ann's mind, for while she made no reply, she had some big inward mental reservations which almost broke the ominous silence as she said to herself, "I guess I work hard enough for them."

Mrs. McKay got very little satisfaction that day, but she did not give up. The next Sunday she pressed Ann to go and hear a Mr. Armstrong Halliday. At this time the Methodists were very much despised and too poor to erect a place of worship; consequently meetings were held in private homes. On this notable Sunday the parlor was crowded and Ann was very glad to be out of range of the minister's eye. She remembered nothing that was said except the text, which was not one that would strike the average sinner. The words were:

24

"But thou, when thou prayest, enter into thy closet, and when thou hast shut the door, pray to thy Father which is in secret; and thy Father which seeth in secret shall reward thee openly" (Matt. 6:6).

Between eight and nine o'clock that evening, after the day's work was finished, Ann made her way up to the attic. It was just a bare room, the only furniture being a large wooden chair. Ann hardly knew why she did it, but she voluntarily knelt for the first time in her life and began to cry out without any conception of what was the matter. She lost all control of herself, and her mistress heard the noise down three flights of stairs. To her daughter she said, "Ann is taking the minister's advice," and a little while after she went up and asked Ann what was the matter. Ann looked up and answered, "I don't know, ma'am." But just then she seemed to have a sudden revelation of her trouble, and she added, "Oh, yes, I do. I see all the sins that ever I did from the time I was five years old all written on the chair in front of me, every one." And then, as she looked down, she cried out, "Oh, ma'am, worse than all, I see hell open ready to swallow me." Then, like one of old, she began to smite her breast, and without any knowledge that she was repeating

Scripture, cried out, "God be merciful to me, a sinner." Once more she became desperate, as she cried over and over again for mercy.

Mrs. McKay tried to hush her up, saying, "Don't let master hear you." She suggested Ann should go to her own room and pray, and said, "I will go to mine and pray for you." But Ann was too much in earnest for this, and said, "I don't care, ma'am, if all the world hears me; I must cry for mercy."

After a little while she retired to her room, but conviction did not cease, and she continued to pray until twelve o'clock, when she jumped up, saying, as she rose, "No mercy, Lord, for me?" But her heart was assured as the question passed her lips, and Ann always said that as she looked up she saw the Saviour as He was on Calvary, and knew right then that His blood atoned for her sins. She had the Methodist way of expressing it when she said, "I felt then something burning in my heart. I just longed for the morning that I could go home and tell my father and mother what the Lord had done for me." She went over to the table and picked up a Testament which the young ladies used, and then prayed her first simple request as a child of God. "O Lord," she said, "you that has taken away this awful burden, intolerable to bear, wouldn't you enable me to read one of these little things?" putting her finger on a verse. The text was, "Whosoever drinketh of this water shall thirst again, but whosoever drinketh of the water that I shall give shall never thirst."

Our readers may believe it or disbelieve it, but for the first time in her life Ann was able to read a verse of Scripture. She did not get the whole verse, but, as our later narrative will show, this was the beginning of Divine assistance in the teaching of an ignorant girl.

The next morning Ann had her first opportunity of testimony. In the first place, she was sent to the tavern for the daily supply of beer for the master. It did not occur to her that this was inconsistent for a Christian, but when she entered the saloon she saw a mother giving her child a drink of whisky. Even the tavern-keeper's wife protested at this, and said, "Don't give that poison to the child." Ann at once stepped up and said, "Well, ma'am, what makes you keep the poison?" The poor woman answered, "I wouldn't have it in the house if I could help it, but I can't, as my husband will sell it." This was Ann's first word of protest against evil.

Later in the day she managed to get home to tell

27

her father and mother of her new-found joy. On the way the tempter suggested, "You don't feel the burning in your heart now. You had better not say anything about it till you are sure." However, she resisted the evil one, and with real fervor broke the news to her parents. They gave her a very cool reception. The only response from her mother was, "Oh, you are like your old grandfather; you are going out of your head." Not very encouraging, this, for a young convert. However, that very day she received a letter from her older sister, Mary, who was working away off in Armagh, and asked her mistress to read it to her. Ann did not remember any news conveyed in the letter except the one statement of her sister: "I am sure you have good news to tell me, Ann. I know by the answer that I got in prayer." This illustrates the power of prayer, for Ann's sister had written the letter two days before. At that time Ann was utterly indifferent to religious influences, but by the time the letter reached her she had undergone the great change and had become a child of God.

4

STUMBLING UPWARDS

"Rejoice not against me, O mine enemy: when I fall, I shall arise."—Micah 7:8.

IN HER EARLY Christian experience Ann was very much the child of circumstances, and her religious life was lived largely in the ebb and flow of feeling. How unsafe it is to base our hopes of heaven or our present relationship to God upon the trivial happenings of everyday life or the changing moods of the human mind. Of course, Ann was not versed in the Word of God, and the only spiritual help she received was at the class meeting, where she listened to the experiences of others, but it could not take the place of thorough instruction in the truth.

As illustrating the kind of evidence that served to buoy up her life at this time, Ann tells the following little incident: One evening she had cleared out the ashes from the fireplace, but instead of leaving them by the grate until the morning, as was her wont, she took them out and set the box on the brick floor of the scullery. In the morning the box and part of the lid had been consumed by the fire, and at once Ann jumped to the conclusion that this was an evidence that she was saved and that God cared for her, for had she not taken the box out that evening the house would have been burned down.

There were evidently two ways of looking at the same thing, for this occurrence led Mr. McKay to discharge her, as he considered her unsafe and not to be trusted.

She had only been in her new situation a few months when Mr. Halliday, the minister under whom she had been converted, having evidently watched her industry, came to her one day and said that one of the best homes in his circuit needed a girl, and if she was prepared to go he would take her to the situation. Ann at once replied, "I will go anywhere, sir, where I can be free to serve the Lord." He took her to Armagh and introduced her to the family of Dr. Reid, with whom she was to spend many eventful years. He agreed to pay her the munificent salary of two dollars a month. Ann used to say quaintly, "The minister married me to Mrs. Reid," for he made Mrs. Reid promise that she would keep Ann as long as she would stay, and made Ann promise that she would stay as long as she would keep her, and concluded by saying, "It will not be long till I want you myself," as he was engaged to be married then. Many a time when dissatisfied and sorely tried with the difficulties of her situation, Ann would pack her little bundle to leave, but the remembrance of her promise always restrained her.

As further illustrating her vacillàting experience at this time, Ann recalls the fact that on one occasion she was so terribly tried that she practically decided to commit suicide. She selected a novel way of death. Her master, Dr. Reid, had bought a very vicious cow, and scarcely anyone dared to go near it. It was always necessary for the man who tended it to accompany Ann while she milked the cow. They kept it about a mile out of town. On the occasion referred to Ann decided that she would slip off to the milking unaccompanied, and expected that the cow would do the rest. To her astonishment, the savage brute stood perfectly quiet while she finished her operation, and started homeward uninjured with her pail of milk. Mrs. Reid had discovered her absence and given the alarm, and was quite astonished when she saw Ann coming toward the house carrying the milk. When asked who held the cow she simply answered, "Nobody". The event encouraged Ann in the thought that God really cared for her, and the next morning she had taken a new lease of life, for when requested to go and milk she refused to go alone.

After Ann had been with Dr. Reid's family for some five years, he decided to go to Canada. He at once began to collect all his back debts. In those days there were no banking facilities and he was compelled to keep all the money in the house. This was quite well known and Ann was very nervous at being left alone in the home. The family went to the watch-night service at the coming of the New Year and Ann was left alone with the baby. The approach to the house was guarded by two large gates, one of iron and the other of very heavy wood, and these were always kept locked. The backyard was surrounded by a very high stone wall, and things generally seemed secure. At twelve o'clock that night Ann heard the iron gate shake, which was the usual sign of Dr. Reid's arrival. She was just about to go out and unlock the gate when she remembered that the service could not possibly be over, and so she sat still. In a few minutes the noise occurred again, and a man climbed over the iron gate. Then, mounting a stack of turf he managed to get over into the garden. Here the potatoes were kept, and he at once began to rob the pit.

When her master came home Ann told them what had occurred, but her mistress made light of it. However, Ann insisted that this was a warning, and so impressed the doctor that he at once had the windows fixed with iron bars, and a large bolt put on the back door leading to the yard. Just two weeks after this, while the doctor was away out in the country attending a patient, Mrs. Reid and Ann were sitting up awaiting his return, when once more the same noise was heard. She was just about to go out with the key when she was suddenly restrained, and said to Mrs. Reid, "O ma'am, that is the very same noise I heard two weeks ago." Her mistress asked, "Is the kitchen door locked?" Ann replied, "No", and with that she turned the key and pushed the long iron bolt across the door. She had hardly taken her hands off when the latch was lifted. Finding the door locked, the intruder evidently thought it to be a simple matter to burst the lock off, and stepping back he threw his full weight upon the door, but owing to the large bolt it would not yield. He tried again and again. The two women were naturally very much afraid. Ann began to pray, but Mrs. Reid suggested she go and call for help. Ann was afraid to venture out at the front door, but when it came to a choice of do-

ing that or staying alone, she decided she would
run for help.

The first place she called at the man would not
come, and she went on to the barracks, but there
was only one soldier in at the time, and he was on
duty and refused to come. Finally she succeeded
in reaching a home where they had not retired, and
a big, burly fellow came out and at once offered
to go with her, taking his revolver. They returned
to the house just in time to meet Dr. Reid coming
home. The would-be robber heard his usual signal
and jumped over the wall, evidently intent on
meeting Dr. Reid alone. However, when he discovered the two men in the darkness he turned and
fled, but not before the doctor recognized him as a
man he had occasionally hired to do odd jobs around
the house.

The next day the man appeared at the doctor's
office and said he was very sorry to hear of the
fright that Mrs. Reid had got the night before. The
doctor, in a very off-hand manner, replied, "Oh,
that's no matter; sure, no one could get in here
anyhow." Thinking the doctor did not identify
him, the man went off, but otherwise Ann always
felt that he had come with other intentions in mind
that day.

It was in May that preparations were completed for their sailing, and Mrs. Reid asked Ann if she would go along with them to Canada. She replied, "Yes, for I can't break my promise to Mr. Halliday."

She went home to bid her parents goodbye. Her father was very much devoted to her, and at once said, "Ann, I can't let you go." But Ann insisted that she must, as she had already promised, and further, said her ticket was already bought. Ann stayed at home all night, and then asked her parents to go a little way with her. After proceeding some distance down the road Ann turned round to address her father, but suddenly he had disappeared to avoid the pain of saying goodbye. Her mother went on as far as Armagh, to where Ann's sister was living. Together they pleaded with Ann to stay at home, but Ann paid no attention to their entreaties. Her mother finally broke down completely, and wept as she said, "O Ann, I just can't let you go." In a very heartless and unfeeling way Ann turned and said, "I will go. Sure, what's the difference? You won't live more than seven or eight years anyway." Many a time did these cruel words come back to Ann in the years that followed. She went on as far as Moy alone. Her mother and sister stood watching her for nearly two miles, and the look on her mother's face haunted her for many a long day.

Even then they did not give up hope, and the next morning mother and sister were outside of the house where Ann was staying. Dr. Reid very kindly offered to release her from her promise, but Ann was obstinate and determined that she would go with them. Finding that it was useless to plead longer, they bade her a last good-bye. Her sister Mary gave her a little verse as they separated. Ann did not understand the force of it at the time, but it often came to her with much blessing in later days. It was Revelation 3:11: "Hold that fast which thou hast, that no man take thy crown." Ann sent back a little memento to her father, which seemed to show a little softening of her heart at the time of separation.

5

FROM OLD WORLD TO NEW WORLD

*"If I take the wings of the morning, and dwell in the
uttermost parts of the sea, even there shall Thy hand
lead me."*—Psalm 139:9, 10.

ANN TOOK SHIP at the river port of Moy. They
were seven weeks on the water, and it must
be remembered that in those early days not only
was the voyage much longer, but the conveniences
were not by any means such as to make an ocean
trip enjoyable. The Reid family numbered seven,
with two other relatives, and Ann had the care of
the whole. There were no ship's cooks or stewards
to minister to their wants. They carried their own
supplies and cooked their own food. Ann had to
serve three families. She says they were all very
seasick. She was the only one that kept well
throughout because, as she said, "Sure, I had no
time to get seasick". She managed to keep around
throughout the whole voyage.

The long journey had its usual incidents and
Ann's duties furnished plenty of opportunity for
unusual annoyances. She had to cook on the ship's
ranges, and when her back was turned her pots

were often set aside, and served the occasion for drawing out her Irish wrath. They dubbed her "the praying-man's biddy", for her master used to hold family worship three times a day, much to the disgust of most of the travellers. Mrs. Reid went up on deck only once during the whole voyage and on that occasion the ship gave a sudden lurch and a poor fellow who was fixing the rigging lost his hold and fell, mangled and dead upon the deck, almost at her feet. The nervous shock, combined with seasickness, kept her in her berth during the rest of the voyage. This all made it much harder for Ann. They met with several severe storms and twice during the journey the passengers were fastened down below. On these occasions the despised praying-man was in great demand. Ann herself thought on one occasion that the end had come, and definitely committed herself to the Lord, expecting with the rest of the passengers that the boat would go down any minute. However, piety prompted by danger is usually evanescent, and as soon as the waves calmed down the passengers returned to their old life of gambling, drinking and swearing.

In our day, with ocean greyhounds to make the voyage so brief, the monotony of the ocean journey is sufficient to make land a welcome sight, and we can well imagine the delight with which, after being seven weeks out of sight of land, the passengers of one of the old sailing vessels would welcome the first glimpse. They entered the port of New York and sailed up the Hudson River. The beautiful scenery there was very refreshing after the ocean journey. From Albany they took the overland route and reached Toronto, then known as Little York. Here they tarried for a few months, and the doctor then moved to Thornhill and took up his practice in that place. The changing circumstances evidently had done little to assist the progress of Ann's religious life. At Thornhill at that period a very excellent lady, Mrs. Phoebe Palmer, led the class in the Methodist church, but while Mrs. Reid was in constant attendance, Ann could hardly be coaxed to go.

After some five years' residence in this place Ann's circumstances were greatly changed by the unexpected death of Mrs. Reid. With this Ann became the general housekeeper and had sole charge of the children. The Christian life of the home at that period was not such as to commend Christ to those who knew anything about it. Dr. Reid was regular in his observance of family worship, and was class leader at the church. Ann, too, professed to be a Christian, but anyone who had seen her in one of the terrible outbreaks of her temper would have questioned the reality of it. It is true the children were annoying. Sometimes when Ann had finished scrubbing the floors they would track right in with their muddy shoes, in spite of her protests; this was more than she could stand and anything but an exhibition of Christian graces followed. Dr. Reid did not always help her in spiritual things; in fact, he sometimes tried her sorely. Ann was expected to look after the horse and buggy, and she had to attend to the robes. The doctor was very particular that these should be brought out at the last minute from the stove, so that they would be nice and warm for the journey. One day he saw her coming back to the house, having fixed the robes in the cutter some time before he expected to start. Evidently annoyed, he pulled Ann's hair as she went past him. Instantly Ann's temper blazed up and, snatching a big stick of wood that lay in the pathway, she threw it at him with all the force at her command. Fortunately it missed its mark. Evidently neither of them was much edified by what followed, for not a word passed between them for the next two weeks, and at family prayer Ann used to put her fingers in her ears to keep out the sound of her master's voice. We do not wonder that at the class meeting Ann was diffident about getting up and giving her experience before Dr. Reid, who led her class and whose duty it was to give the young Christians fatherly advice and Christian counsel after they had narrated their experience. We cannot wonder that Ann was aggravated when the doctor used to conclude her narration by quoting an old Methodist hymn that ran thus:

> *"Your faith by holy tempers prove,*
> *By actions show your sins forgiven,*
> *And seek the glorious things above,*
> *And follow Christ, your head, to heaven."*

In spite of these untoward happenings, Ann did not give up the struggle to do that which was right, but she describes her life at this period as truly awful, sinning and repenting, sinning and repenting. She knew nothing of abiding rest. She used to often quote, when referring to this time, the little song that ran:

> " 'Tis worse than death my God to love,
> And not my God alone."

However, through her struggles a kind hand was guiding her on to a place where she should not only enjoy greater blessing, but bear sweeter fruit.

6

DEFEAT TO VICTORY, OR THE SECOND GREAT CHANGE

"O wretched man that I am, who shall deliver me? I thank God through Jesus Christ."—Rom. 7:24, 25.

AMONG OUR READERS we doubt not there will be wide diversity of view in theological matters, and even with those who have the assurance of salvation there will be great differences of opinion as to the expressions to be used to describe various phases of Christian experience. As the unhappy contentions in the Church of Christ have rarely conduced to edification, it is not the purpose of this book to enter into controversial themes.

However, we come to describe a great change in this life under consideration, and we do not wish to be misunderstood. A numerous body of Christians believe that Christian life can be divided into two distinct stages, the one summed up under the word "justification," and the other and further experience under the term "sanctification". In defining these states, however, great diversity of opinion is expressed. Some maintain that sanctification is something only to be experienced in the future state. Then among those who believe that sanctification is the present privilege of the Christian, two different views prevail—some contending that the experience consists in the entire eradication of the "old Adamic nature", while others contend that it is the state in which inward evil tendencies are entirely controlled or suppressed—but in the contention the one side too often gives evidence that there is need of a more perfect eradication, and the other that there is room for a more complete suppression. In this narrative, therefore, we are not contending for a theory, but simply narrating facts, and are frank to admit that we have witnessed the practical results, which we are about to set forth, in the lives of Christians taking either view of this great doctrine. In a general way we can appeal to our readers, and feel confident they will admit that in the circle of their acquaintances there are two classes of Christians. In the one there is not much to attract those who have never tasted of Christian joys. They live all too much under the cloud. It is true that they struggle to do right, and that there has been certainly a great change from their former life. They witness that their sins are forgiven. With actual wrongs committed there is speedy confession and repentance. They acknowledge their own powerlessness in the presence of temptation, and admit that they too often yield to some special besetment.

On the other hand, there is another class whose life and presence seems attractive. It is characterized by joyous victory. The soul has unbroken fellowship heavenward, and with its peace and joy it carries blessing wherever its influence is felt. The will is surrendered and the life wholly consecrated and the Divine acceptance is sealed by the filling of the Spirit. We shall not quarrel here as to how the transition is made from one state to the other. That those who have lived in the one should pass out of the first and into the second is sufficient for us. In other words, that the life of victory is possible by grace, is all that we desire to maintain.

In the case of Ann, who had been schooled among the Methodists, we cannot wonder that she largely dropped into their phraseology and more or less felt the impression of the teaching that prevailed. However, up to this time she knew very little of the teaching of John Wesley, and did not understand his theory of sanctification, and still less had she any corresponding experience. Her ungovernable temper was her great besetment. She wept over it, confessed it, fought it, but all too frequently the whole process had to be repeated in the face of some great outbreak under specially trying circumstances. There came a change, however, and a time when she was delivered from its slavery.

It happened thus: A young man who stayed all night at the Reid home, before retiring led the family worship, reading Psalm 34. The 16th verse was strongly impressed upon Ann's mind: "The face of the Lord is against them that do evil, to cut off the remembrance of them from the earth." She requested the young man to mark it for her, and then went to her room and knelt down and prayed for light. She opened the Bible at the place where the leaf had been turned down, but the adversary was there to contend with her. His first suggestion was, "You can't read it", to which Ann replied, "Well, the Lord will give it to me," and in a wonderful way she was enabled to read it over and over again. Men may explain it as they will, but with the exception of the night of her conversion Ann had never been able to read a word or decipher the alphabet, but from this time forth she could read in a simple way from the Bible, although until toward the close of her life she was unable to read any other book, and a newspaper was like a foreign language to her. While still upon her knees she said, "Lord, what

45

is evil?" And the answer came, "Anger, wrath, malice," etc. All night long she wept and prayed as the inward sinfulness was revealed to her. Toward morning, in sheer desperation, she cried out, "O Lord, how will I know when I get deliverance?" The answer came, "Well, Jacob wrestled until he prevailed." In her simplicity Ann asked, "What does 'prevailed' mean?" and to her the reply came, "Getting just what you come for and all you want." Again she queried, "And what will it do for me when I get it?" The reply came back, "It will enable you to rejoice evermore, pray without ceasing, and in everything give thanks. You will live above the troubles of this world and the things that now upset you."

But other suggestions were interpolated from another source. Like a flash she recalled the circumstances of former outbreaks, and the suggestion came, "Yes, just wait until you are scrubbing the floor and the children come in with their dirty feet—then you will see." But the conviction deepened that these outbreaks of the carnal mind were displeasing to God, and that there was deliverance from them. When the morning broke and the children began to awaken, she was almost fleeing back to the bush to continue in her waiting for deliverance. She said determinedly, "I'll die, but I'll have it." She arose and went downstairs. To her over-wrought mind the personal struggle with the adversary was so great that she thought she could hear him following her. In the parlor she met the young man whose word had reached her heart. He asked her what she had been crying for all night, to which she replied, "I want to be sanctified throughout body, soul and spirit." He simply said, "Well, Ann, how were you justified?" She replied, "Why, just by believing what God said." "Well," he said, "complete victory comes in the same way."

Again Ann went to prayer and pleaded the promise, "Ask and it shall be given you, seek and ye shall find, knock and it shall be opened unto you." She cried, "Lord, I have been knocking all night: Open unto me! Open unto me!" And there is little doubt but that the answer came there and then. For two years it seemed to her as though she had entered heaven. This time the family were aroused with her shouts of praise instead of her cries and groans. She said, as she looked out, that nature took on a different hue, and the very trees seemed to be clapping their hands and praising God. With her heart overflowing she cried, "Father, didn't you intend that man should praise you more than these?"

She at once began to tell it around. She went to her old class leader and made known her new-found joy. He bade her to rejoice evermore, and pray without ceasing in order to keep it. This brought in a shade of doubt, as she wondered how she could pray without ceasing. She thought of the absorbing affairs of life and the things that would occupy her mind, and wondered how such a thing was possible. But her mind was speedily set at rest by the Scripture passage, "Not slothful in business, fervent in spirit, serving the Lord."

Her joy was so great that she could not eat, and for eight days was without food. Friends tried to persuade her to break her fast and to go forth and give her testimony, but it was some time before she felt that she could return to the ordinary duties.

For seven years and a half after this it just seemed as though she were living in heavenly places. She fell back on the Methodist hymnal for expression, as she often cried:

"The opening heavens round me shine
With streams of sacred bliss,
While Jesus shows His presence mine
And whispers 'I am His'."

48

At the first dawn of consciousness in the morning her mouth was filled with praises and her hands clapping for joy. There was very little difficulty in maintaining her Christian life with such a joyous experience. One morning, however, she awoke and instead of the usual sense of joy and the burst of praise, her lips were dumb. At once the temptation came, "You have lost the blessing." While thus tried, she fell asleep again and dreamed that she was talking to another woman with a like experience, and in her dream Ann urged her to walk by faith, quoting the text, "But the just shall live by faith," and urged her just to trust God. With that she awoke and turned the sermon upon herself, with the resultant obtainment of perfect peace of mind.

7

A NEW NAME

"Thou shalt be called by a new name . . . thou shalt no more be termed Forsaken . . . but thou shalt be called Hephzibah."—Isaiah 62:2, 4.

WHEN JACOB had finished his all-night experience during which Jehovah broke the power of the carnal life within him, and brought him to the place of helplessness, where he could only cling to God and plead for blessing, he received a new name which described the changed life upon which he then entered. It is not to be wondered at that the life whose record we are now writing should at this time of wonderful change call for a new name. Just what length of time elapsed ere she received it we do not know. At first it was a term of derision. The Catholic boys scribbled in chalk-marks upon her door, "Holy Ann lives here. Go in and have a word of prayer". Gradually this term of derision clung to her, and even friends began to call her by the name. In her simple way, when she could no longer check the application of the word to her, she went to her closet and cried, "Oh, Father, they are calling me Holy Ann. Make me holy, so that the children will not be telling lies." By degrees this new name was so generally applied that for many years the greater number of her friends in all communities of Christians could not tell her proper name.

Some may demur at the acceptance of such a title, as though it involved spiritual pride, but we feel confident that were such a term to be applied to them its effect would be that of humiliation. It certainly did not cause Ann to become puffed up, although it did cause her, with the whole purpose of her life, to desire to fulfil the command of God, "Be ye holy, for I am holy". From this time forth there can be little doubt that the whole tenor of her life was changed, and wherever she went she became a faithful witness for God and an inspiration to all who knew her.

8

POWER IN PRAYER

*"Whatsoever we ask we receive of Him, because we keep
His commandments and do the things that are pleasing
in His sight."*—1 John 3:22.

THIS POOR, ignorant woman had stepped from a
life of struggling, marked too often by defeat,
into a life of power and blessing—power not only
manward, but into a life of wonderful intimacy
with God and prevailing prayer. It was not long
before this became generally recognized, and
weaker Christians sought her counsel and begged
her prayers, for it was very plainly seen that she
had entered into the place where in a marvellous
way she could "ask and receive", and where she
had become a special subject of the thoughtful care
of her Heavenly Father.

There was one incident that she has often told
which in some directions has been received with
doubt and skeptical unbelief, which beautifully
illustrates this. We are confident that the facts are
just as narrated. In jumping over a fence she
twisted her foot and injured the ankle. It got worse
and worse, until finally she was unable to keep

around on it any longer. Dr. Reid said it would be necessary to scrape the bone. In these days, when such care is taken to relieve pain, we wonder how it was possible that Ann submitted to this painful operation without any anæsthetic, but, as she said, the Lord sustained her. It was a long, long time before the wound healed up, and for over a year Ann was unable to walk. During this time of enforced inactivity she learned many precious lessons. She had become very weak through the great strain upon her system, and one day the doctor ordered her fresh eggs and milk. It did not occur to him that he was giving an impossible prescription, for it was in the dead of winter, and not a fresh egg was to be had anywhere in the village. All these matters were made subjects of prayer by Ann, who was learning already that the things impossible with man are possible with God. She was sitting in her chair shortly after this, between the kitchen door and the back stairway. The door having been left ajar, to her surprise a hen came in and dropped down at Ann's feet. Something said to her, "Lift it up and put it on the first step of the stair." Intuitively Ann recognized that her Father was about to meet her need. The hen went upstairs, and in her simple way Ann asked that it might not be permitted to cackle, lest Dr.

Reid's daughters should hear it. (In the village at that time there was another unique character who was the laughing-stock of the boys because she permitted the hens to live in her house, and Ann did not want to be likened to old Peggy Casey.) After a few minutes the hen came down very quietly and Ann reached to the door and let her out.

Then another great difficulty faced her. She had not put any weight on her foot for a long time. It was impossible for her to walk, and while she was confident that the doctor's prescription had been filled at the top of the stairs, she did not know how she was to obtain it. She prayed, and felt that the answer came, "Go up for it." But in her simple way she said, "Father, how can I? It is impossible." Some time before this she had learned a little refrain which she had taken as one of the motto verses of her life. It ran like this:

> *"Faith, mighty faith, the promise sees,*
> *And looks to God alone,*
> *Laughs at impossibilities*
> *And cries, 'It shall be done.'"*

When she spoke of impossibilities the inward voice said, "Well, say your verse." She hesitated for some time, but at last faith conquered and she re-

peated the simple words. Then she received her
instructions as to how she was to act. She worked
her chair toward the door, and then, sitting on the
first step, she raised herself with her hands, step
after step, until she had reached the top. The hen
had laid the egg in an old box just at the head of
the stair, and she was able to reach it without getting off the top step. But how was she to get down
with the egg in her hand? In her simple way—
for she used to pray about all these little things in a
very familiar manner—she asked for directions,
and the word came, "Put it in your pocket". She
then managed to descend in the same fashion, and
was just safely back in her chair when Paddy, the
servant, walked in. Ann prayed, "Now, Father,
don't let him ask me where I got it," and in response
to her simple faith he took the egg without a word
and fixed it for her without making any enquiry.
This is the more surprising when it is stated that
he had been all through the village in his endeavour
to secure eggs for Ann.

For three weeks the hen returned every day
without making the slightest noise. At the end of
this time the doctor one morning said she did not
need any more milk and eggs, and recommended
beef tea instead. Just after this one of the young
ladies came in, and the hen, disturbed, came cack-

ling downstairs. The young woman was very much
startled, and said, "What, Ann, have you got hens
upstairs like old Peggy Casey?" And as the hen
came cackling down, the young girl shooed it out
into the yard and it never returned. Afterwards
when Ann was able to get out again she tried to
single out this one in order to show it special kindness, but was unable to do so. When in her customary way she appealed to her Father to show her
which one it was, she heard the voice speaking to
her inward consciousness, and telling her, "My
glory will I not give to another". For a long time
Ann hesitated to speak of this incident, but her
diffidence in telling of God's goodness was reproved,
for she heard Him say, "I fed you just as really as
I fed Elijah through the ravens, and yet you are
ashamed to make it known."

Some time after her experience with the hen
Ann was away from home visiting some friends
in the country. She ventured to tell them how her
Father had provided for her in her sickness. The
lady of the house expressed her unbelief, but Ann
said quietly, "Well, my Father will make you believe it before I go." And sure enough He did. Ann
had not the money to take her home, and one morning as she knelt in prayer she asked her Father
how much it would cost, and had just received the

answer when the door opened and the lady of the house stood there. Ann said, "Oh, come in, till I see if you can count as well as my Father." She came in and reckoned up the mileage and what the fare would be, and it was exactly the same amount as that which Ann had been told. Then the woman said, "Do you think you will get it, Ann?" She replied, "To be sure I shall. I am sure of it, for the silver and the gold are my Father's, and the cattle upon a thousand hills, and I am sure He will send it to me." That morning she started out with the woman's mother to spend the day. She had only been away about half an hour when a man called and asked for the "shouting girl". The woman said, "She has just gone out for the day," and then she added in an amused way, "Do you know, she was praying this morning for money to take her back home, and she says she is sure her Father will send it." "Well," said the man, "and so am I, for I have it here in my pocket." He then told her how he had been impressed to give her the amount, and had been sent around with it. The woman was astonished, and when she saw Ann returning that evening she ran out to meet her and at once proceeded to tell her the good news. In a quiet, matter-of-fact way Ann said, "Didn't I tell you? I knew my Father would send it to me.

You remember you wouldn't believe about the egg, and I told you my Father would make you believe before I left. So now this has come for you." In order to avoid the point of the remark the woman said, "Well, give me the money then, if it has come for me," but quickly Ann replied, "No, the money was sent for me, but the lesson is for you."

It must not be thought, however, that Ann's prayers were always selfish. She had a large heart for the needs of others. Every spring she used to make two barrels of soft soap—one for their own use, and always one for the poor. On one occasion she had made the one barrelful and was at the last kettleful of the second, when something seemed to go wrong and it would not thicken. The children came out to see how she was getting along, and of course, child-like, they wanted to know what was the matter with the soap. In her familiar way Ann said, "My Father says it only needs a bone." They asked, "Well, haven't you got one?" She said, "No, but my Father bids me wait till morning." "But suppose it should rain in the night? The water would spoil it more." But Ann quietly said, "My Father said wait till the morning, and I will wait, and cover it up now." By three o'clock the next morning Ann was up and out to see her soap. There by the side of the kettle lay a large marrow bone, from which the meat had all been taken, but which had not been boiled. With her quiet "Thank you", Ann lifted up her heart in praise, and then, picking up the axe, proceeded to break the bone and put it in the soap, and in a short time it had the desired effect. The children were very anxious to see the outcome of Ann's faith. Her calm confidence in these matters had already produced an effect in the home, and they somehow expected to see Ann's prayers answered. When, in reply to their query, she said that the bone had come, "It was here by the kettle when I came out," one of the children said, "Oh, I guess a dog dropped the bone there." Like a flash Ann retorted, "I don't care if the devil brought it; my Father sent it."

As showing her interest and sympathy with others, another incident is told which was well verified at the time. The Salvation Army had opened up a station in the village and Ann became interested in them. She found on enquiry that the officers in charge were really in actual need. She asked some friends with whom she was staying if they ever took them in any food. They replied that they had on several occasions, but added, "We haven't very much to give." Ann asked the woman if she would not take them some eggs, but the response was that the hens were not laying then. Ann said, "Well, but if I ask my Father for them, will you give them to the officers?" The woman replied, "Yes, I will."

Ann went to prayer, and shortly afterwards she proceeded to the barn and gathered over a dozen eggs. The woman was amazed, and wanted to know where she got them, but Ann would not satisfy her curiosity in the matter. As bearing upon this incident, it is a significant fact that this woman years afterwards sent in to the city to request Ann's prayers.

Of course, in many of these incidents one may find a natural explanation, and we are not trying to narrate these experiences with the thought that a miracle was wrought in every instance. God frequently uses natural things in order to answer the prayers of His children. Of course, some may say that the things all happened by chance, but it is certainly a most convenient chance that always appears to meet the needs of those who cry unto God.

Ann tells how, shortly after she was able to get around after her long sickness, when she was still using her crutches somewhat, and it was most difficult to get to meetings, special services were started in the church, and Ann sought to get out on every occasion. She was always eager to assist, and ever anxious to lead souls to Christ. One morning, when Ann got up, to her dismay she noticed that there had been a heavy fall of snow. She at once said, "Oh, Father, now I can't go to the meeting tonight. Won't you please send someone to make a path for me?" At that time there was no man in the house, and the building was nearly a quarter of a mile back from the road.

On several other occasions, in answer to her prayers, someone had been sent along to shovel snow, but this day, after Ann's prayer, she heard the girls laughing, and one said to the other, "Come and see what is making the path for Ann." When Ann looked out there were five horses going up the avenue one after the other as straight as a line. They ran up and down in colt fashion no less than four times, until there was a perfectly beaten track all through the deep snow. As soon as they got out on the road, however, they began to scatter, but up the avenue they had made a regular, straight track. Ann tells how she enjoyed the meeting that night, and to those who gathered there told with beaming face how God had opened her way through the snow.

9

THE STORY OF THE WELL

"He gave them drink abundantly, as out of the depths."
—Psalm 78:15.

ONE OF THE MOST remarkable answers to prayer in Ann's experience was that in which she obtained water in a dry well. This incident has been told and re-told scores of times, with all sorts of variations and additions. I was most careful to get the full particulars and surrounding circumstances taken down as Ann narrated it. The event occurred in the long, dry weeks of summer.

During this period the well at their home was usually dry for two or three months, and the boys were compelled to haul water in barrels from a well about half a mile away. This was very hard work, and especially when they had to provide, not only for household needs, but for the stock as well. One evening at the close of the day Ann was sitting in the kitchen with the boys around her, telling them some of the remarkable ways in which her Heavenly Father had answered her prayers. When she had just concluded one of these narratives, Henry said, "Ann, why don't you ask

your Father to send water in that well, and not
have us boys work so hard? I was down in the well
looking at it today, and it is just as dry as the
floor." This was thrown out to Ann in a half-
joking, half-earnest way, as though to challenge
her faith. He little dreamt of the serious way that
Ann would take it.

When she got up into her little room that night
she knelt in prayer and said, "Now, Father, you
heard what Henry said tonight. If I get up in
class meeting and say, 'My God shall supply all
your needs according to his riches in glory by
Christ Jesus', the boys won't believe I am what I
profess to be if you don't send the water in the
well." She then continued to plead that the water
might be sent, and finally, rising from her knees,
she said, "Now, Father, if I am what I profess to
be, there will be water in the well in the morning."
When she came down the next morning Henry was
out preparing to go for the water as usual. To his
surprise and great amusement he saw Ann take
up the two pails and start for the well. He watched
her from the kitchen window as she hooked the
pail to the windlass and began to lower it. If she
had done it the night before it would have gone
with a bang to the bottom, but after a while there

was a splash, and still down the pail went, and
Ann began with difficulty to wind up the windlass
again, and at last put the pail upon the well-stand
full of water. She repeated this, and with both
pails full of clear, sparkling water, she walked up
to the house.

And who could wonder that there was a little
air of victory as she set the pails down and said
to Henry, "Well, what do you say now?" To her
surprise he simply answered, "Well, why didn't
you do that long ago, and have saved us all that
work?"

Meditation upon that question, thrown out so
thoughtlessly by this young boy, might yield some
very profitable results. How often we go hungry
and thirsty, suffering the lack of all sorts of needed
things, when a full supply might be ours! "We
have not, because we ask not." Years after a friend
visited the well and was told that from the time
referred to here the well had never been known
to be dry summer or winter.

10

DAILY NEEDS — AND GOD!

*"All things, whatsoever ye pray, and ask for, believe
that ye have received them and ye shall have them."*
—Mark 11:24.

I T WILL BE IMPOSSIBLE for many Christians to
understand the intimacy and familiarity with
which Ann addressed the Divine Being. To some
it will sound almost irreverent—yea, we question
whether there are not those who would think it
blasphemous to speak in the simple way that Ann
was accustomed to do of her Heavenly Father.
Further, we know there are those who would protest against bringing the thousand and one little
matters of everyday life into the sphere of prayer.
It was quite a common thing for Ann to go around
at her daily tasks talking as familiarly to the
Heavenly Father about every little thing as she
would talk to any other person that might be in
the home. Moreover, she sought guidance in every
little detail of life.

That she received special answers, those who
lived with her have no doubt. Even the children
in their play would run to Ann for a solution of

the little difficulties that arose. One of the boys on one occasion had lost a spade, and was dreading the wrath of his father when he should discover that the article was missing. In his distress he went to Ann and appealed to her to ask her Father about it. She at once in her simple way closed her eyes and said, "Father, where is it?" We cannot explain how she understood, or in what form these answers made themselves known to her consciousness, but she immediately made a bee-line for the back of the garden, where the spade was lying hidden in the grass. This was not by any means an isolated case. The children would come to her when their toys were lost, and invariably after Ann had prayed she would at once go to where the missing article was lying.

Only on one occasion did she fail to get her answer about such things, and this exception happened thus: A young minister was visiting the home and was out on the lawn playing croquet with the girls. Ann did not approve of this; at least she did not think it was right for the minister to be spending his time in that way. In her blunt way she asked if he could keep his mind stayed upon God while he was doing this. He replied, "Oh, yes, for a little while." As the game proceeded, one of the young ladies lost a much-prized locket. However, she was quite unconcerned and said, "Oh, never mind. Ann will soon find it for me." She came in and said, "Ann, get it for me now, quick." Ann, in her usual way, went to her Father, but no answer came. She went out to look for it, but could not find it, and it was never found.

Many, many years after she had left the Reid family she came to live at our home. The boys had heard a great deal about Ann's wonderful experiences, and naturally expected to see some demonstration. They hardly liked at first to ask Ann to demonstrate these things, but they used to hide things which Ann would need to use, and then watch to see how she would find them. Perhaps some article of clothing would be put in the most out-of-the-way place they could think of, and then they would watch for the time when Ann would need to use it. Being perfectly ignorant of what had occurred, she would go up to her room or walk up to a corner with her eyes closed, and in her simple way she would say, "Father, where is it?" and after standing a moment or two in silence she would turn around and go direct to the spot where the thing was hidden.

We do not profess to explain this; we simply

narrate what has occurred over and over again. At one place the boys hid the cat and Ann was asked where it was. She had no idea of what had been done, but in her simple way she looked up in prayer, and then made straight for the stove and opened the oven door, when the cat at once jumped out.

Of course in a Christian home such things would not occur very often to satisfy mere idle curiosity. It was not long before those who knew her felt it was too solemn a thing to be thus dealt with. However, in times of need there was never any question as to the fact of Ann's prayers being answered. On one occasion she had risen in the morning, and, as usual, had asked her Father for a verse with which to start the day. The special portion that was given to her was, "And we know that all things work together for good to them that love God". It came while they were at family prayer, and Ann said, "And we will see it before night, too. God will show it."

All through the day Ann watched, but nothing unusual happened. However, when the girls returned from meeting that night Ann asked if they had had a good meeting. One of them answered, "Why, how could we when I lost all the money I had to live on next week on the way there?" Then they told how the money had been lost and they had looked for it all the evening with a lantern.

Before they retired, at the family altar Ann reminded her Father of the promise of the morning, and asked that He would keep the money for her wherever it was. Early in the morning she was awakened with the instruction, "Arise and get the money that you gave Me to keep for you last night." Then came the other voice: "Nonsense! Your leg is too bad for you to get up and go." She did not obey at once and was just falling to sleep when again the voice spoke, bidding her to arise She went out and walked down the path, not looking specially for it, but all at once she was stopped by her Father and she saw a bill lying almost hidden with the snow, by the side of a small hill. She picked it up and took it across the road, where her friend, Mrs. Hughes, lived. Rapping at the door, she said, "Get up and see if this is a bill." The lady took the bill and looked at it in amazement, and said, "This is a five-dollar bill." Ann said, "Come and let us praise the Lord for this." After prayer Ann went back home, and going in, threw the bill down and said, "There; there is your money." The girls looked at it in surprise, for they had searched so long for it. Then they said, "Oh, Ann, don't tell it in class meeting, or people will think we were so careless."

11

A WONDERFUL TEACHER

*"Thou didst hide these things from the wise and prudent,
and didst reveal them unto babes."*—Matt. 11:25.

REFERENCE has been made in other places to the
fact that in a very strange and supernatural
way Ann was taught to read. There are those
who imagine that God never interferes in secular
matters. The course of human wisdom is to them
the only course along which events must move.
We do not wonder at this. We think that the early
disciples found it very hard to believe or enter into
much that the Lord taught, because it was contrary
to their natural wisdom, not did they easily recog-
nize that He understood not only spiritual truth
but temporal matters, in a way that they could
not. We imagine that it was with much hesitation
that Peter bowed to the supremacy of the Lord in
matters that concerned his own special calling.
From childhood Peter had been occupied in the
fishing industry. His father was a fisherman. He
had spent much of his life upon the water. He
doubtless thought that he knew all that was worth
knowing with regard to fishing, the best places and

the best methods to adopt, and after toiling all night long and catching nothing, to his natural mind there would doubtless be something presumptuous in the suggestion that the nets be let down once more for a draft. Listen as he remonstrates, "We have toiled all night and caught nothing." Nevertheless, we know how much of faith there was possibly hidden in that word and inward wondering whether perhaps the Christ was going to show His special power on this occasion. "Nevertheless, at Thy bidding we will let down the net." Peter learned the lesson that even in the common, everyday matters the Lord Jesus understood better than any human mind could.

We know that many will have their doubts as we record God's dealings with Ann in the matter of instruction in so-called secular things. We have recorded how after attending school for some days the teacher gave up, after striving in vain in a hopeless effort to teach Ann the letters of the alphabet. We have further remarked that, at the time of her conversion, in a strange way she was enabled to read one verse from the Word of God to bring comfort and strength to her heart. Still later, at the time when she yielded absolutely to the Lord and was filled with His Spirit, was she enabled to make out a special verse that had brought light and help to her soul. Without any human intervention this process of instruction continued until Ann could read her Bible anywhere and everywhere. In the early stage it seemed almost as though, apart from the letters, she understood the words, but in her later years she was enabled to spell out the words. The most remarkable thing, however, about the whole thing was that Ann to the very close of life was utterly unable to read any other book. We remember on one occasion putting a paper before her and seeing her trying in vain to decipher some of the smallest words. She found it an impossible task. Finally she put her finger on one word and said, "That seems to be 'lord,'" but I don't think it is my Lord, as my heart doesn't burn when I see it." The writer then looked over the paper and found her finger upon the word indicated, but noticed that it was a report regarding the South African war, in which it spoke of Lord Roberts' achievements. We do not attempt to explain at all this strange phenomenon, but we do know on the testimony of many credible witnesses that it was so. Both in public and in private Ann could freely, not to say fluently, read from the Word of God, and it was marvellous the way the truth would flow forth from her lips when speaking at her Father's bidding.

While she found it utterly impossible to memorize Scripture, yet she made it so constantly her meat and drink that the Holy Spirit could bring to her remembrance just the passage suited to the occasion. A great many can testify to the aptness and point of the Scriptures that Ann would give on different occasions. It was quite a common thing for Christian people visiting the home to request Ann to ask her Father for a verse for them, and in a wonderful way, after lifting up her eyes and her heart heavenward, Ann would give forth some passage which was evidently most suited to the special need; in fact, without knowing the circumstances, she became over and over again the medium for the Divine voice either to guide, comfort or to correct those who thus sought her ministry.

12

"TO YOUR REMEMBRANCE"

"He shall teach you all things, and bring to your remembrance all that I said unto you."—John 14:26.

IT IS SOMETIMES difficult to understand the contradictions of life. In the case of Ann there are those who would imagine that she had a wonderful memory, simply because she was always pouring forth Scripture verses; in fact, the Scriptures were woven into her every day phraseology and she seemed to express herself more readily in Bible language than in any other way. To some who knew her gift in this matter it may come as a surprise to know that one of Ann's sorest trials in the early days was her lack of memory, and to the end of her life she always protested that she had no natural memory. If she desired a verse of Scripture to bear upon a certain line she would walk over to a corner of the room and with uplifted heart she would ask her Father for a suitable portion, and the word would be given her and she would tell it out, often with wonderful power and an aptness that everyone had to acknowledge.

In her early life she had a great desire to memorize Scripture verses. One day she tried for an hour to get a verse, but she found it impossible to remember it. The next day she went to a friend, who requested her to stay with the baby while she went down town. Ann took charge and then prayed that the child might sleep during the whole time of her friend's absence so that she might once more try to learn her verse. She got a New Testament and went over and over the same verse again, but without success. Finally it seemed as though the voice spoke to her and asked, "Ann, what is the matter with you?" Ann replied, "Well, I never saw the like of me. I spell and spell, but can't remember a word," and she broke out crying.

Then the voice spake again, "Well, I thought Christ was a satisfying portion—all in all to you?" Ann replied, "Well, Father, I would like to remember these verses." Her Father said, "What do you want to get that message for?" Ann replied, "Well, the class leader always quotes it in his prayer, and I like it." The special verse she was trying to memorize was, "Whatsoever ye desire, when ye pray believe that ye receive it and ye shall have it." The reply came back again, "Did you ever see a mother send a child on an errand and observe that the child forgot it before it got half way to its destination? Well, you would be just the same. But I will give it to you just when I want you to have it, and then you won't have time to forget."

This seemed to satisfy Ann in a measure, but she then in a persistent way said, "Won't you teach me the little things on the doors?" She could never tell the numbers of a house. The voice replied, "Why do you want to be able to read them?" She said, "So that I could go around by myself." Then came the answer, "No, for then you would go to places where they do not want you. I will always take you myself or send a pilot." Ann was so ignorant that she did not know the meaning of this last word, but the next morning a woman came for her to go and pray with her mother, who was dying, and she was instructed to go with this pilot and then Ann understood.

I shall never forget my own experience with Ann in this line. She had been invited by my parents to come and live with us permanently, and I was deputed to return with Ann to the city while she collected her belongings. I was a perfect stranger in the city, and in consequence was of no service in finding the location of places. She had left her things here, there and all over, and she could neither tell the names of the persons or streets, nor the numbers of the houses. Here and there she would recall possibly a name, and on some occasions would remember the street.

We set out one morning to visit the places where she had left different articles of clothing. I carried her suit-case. She could not tell me where she was going first, but we would walk along the street, and suddenly Ann would stop and ask her Father which way to turn. I was not used to praying on street corners, and frankly confess that I felt at times embarrassed and somewhat ashamed to be in Ann's company.

To find the first house we at last went into a store. Ann had the name of the person given to her, but did not know where she lived. The store-keeper was busy, but said that she had moved and was living on such and such a street, and gave the number. Seeing that I was a stranger he said he would write down the street and number for us. As he turned around for a pencil Ann said, "Father, don't let him find it." After looking for some time he came back and said, "Well, that is strange. I had a pencil here just a little while ago but I can't find it. I guess I will put on my hat and go out with you and show you the place." This simplified matters in the first call.

At the next place Ann could not remember the name of the individual, and evidently did not know the house. Several times as we walked on she said, "That looks like the house," but was directed to go past. Finally, she stopped and said, "My Father says this is the house." I said, "Well, Ann, you can go up and see; I am not going."

It seemed to me too ridiculous to ring the doorbell and meet people without knowing whom you wanted to see or where they lived. With perfect confidence Ann went up and rang the bell, and when the people came, turned around in a kind of triumphant way and beckoned for me to come up.

This kind of experience was repeated over and over again that day. It was at first very mortifying to me, and then to further complicate matters Ann wanted me to go that night to the Salvation Army with her. I finally agreed to go along and when opportunity was given for testimony Ann jumped up and in a joyful way began to praise her Father for the way He had led that day and guided her aright, and then turning to me and directing all attention upon me she said, "She was afraid to trust my Father. She wouldn't believe that the Lord could guide me to the right

79

houses," and then concluded by turning and saying to me, "Now, you get up and speak."

I leave the reader to imagine my feelings as I arose to confess my unbelief and how humiliated and embarrassed I had been several times that day but I certainly had learned that Ann had a strange power and that she had such intimate guidance as I had never seen demonstrated before.

13

PROVIDENTIAL PROTECTION

"The angel of the Lord encampeth round about them that fear Him and delivereth them."—Psalm 34:7.

IN HER LONG CAREER Ann had quite a number of very narrow escapes, and there were several occasions on which it seemed as though the powers of evil had designed either to destroy her life or rob her of virtue. On one occasion Ann was out in the bush gathering some wood, as she did not care to trouble anyone else to do it. In a very lonely part a man suddenly appeared, and after watching her, asked why she was gathering wood, and why her husband did not do that kind of work for her. Innocently Ann answered, "I have no husband. I am joined to the Lord." Looking around in every direction, he asked, "How far is it to the nearest house?" "Oh," Ann said, "it is a good way off." Then, as though restrained, he said, "Well, if you come down tomorrow I will bring a big load of wood here, but don't come till after dark." Quite innocently Ann promised that she would come for it. That night she received a warning dream, in which the evil intentions of

81

the man were revealed, and Ann was saved from what was evidently a snare prepared for her.

Many years afterward, while visiting in the lower section of the city, she was asked by a friend to call at a certain house which was notorious as a den of vice. When Ann entered the door she recognized in the man who kept the place the very one who had met her in the bush years ago, and one of the women that was with him immediately recognized Ann. The old lady at once knelt down in that sinful place and prayed for them. As she confessed, she was very glad to get out of it once more.

On another occasion Ann was alone in the house. She had finished her churning on this particular morning, and carried the buttermilk downstairs, but instead of taking it through into the milk cellar, she put it just at the foot of the steps, intending, as her custom was, to clean out the cellar first. Ann, in her usual way, was talking to her Father, and said she was coming back to finish this work later on. After dinner, when she was left alone, she proceeded to wash up the dishes, and then, noticing a small hole in the carpet, she said, "I will mend this, Father, before I go down in the cellar to clean."

While thus engaged a man entered their lane and came toward the house. Ann paid little heed to him, but proceeded with her work. She said that he turned aside into the hedge for a little while, and when he came out had his arm in a sling. While she was working on the carpet he suddenly appeared in the doorway and asked for help. Ann said, "I have nothing." "Where are the girls?" he queried. Ann said, "They are gone out for the afternoon and won't be back till evening." "Where's the men?" "Back in the bush," she said. "How far away is that?" he continued. "About half a mile," Ann said.

Satisfied that there was no one around, he asked her if she could get him a drink of buttermilk, knowing that she would have to go to the cellar for it. Ann said, "Yes, sir, I can," and at once proceeded down the steps. Her Father said, "Be quick", and then Ann began to be afraid. She ran with all her might to the foot of the stairs and dipped into the crock for a drink and rushed up again, but not until the man had made his way and stood at the top of the steps. However, her sudden return with the can in her hand seemed to so surprise him that he backed away from the cellarway and then took the milk. After he had

83

taken a drink Ann again kneeled down to finish mending the hole. The man sat down and asked Ann if she would mend a small tear in his trousers. The man had torn it in going into the hedge to tie up his arm in a sling. She did not know what to do, and so in order to gain time she proceeded with the thread and needle to carry out his wish, praying all the while that the Lord would take care of her. She was convinced that the man intended robbery. Ere she had finished getting the needle and thread, to her great relief she heard the windlass creaking at the well, and at once jumped up and said, "Oh, there is Mr. Reid now, sir." But the man evidently did not want to meet him, and slunk away, trembling, Ann said, as though he had the palsy. She felt that God had delivered her.

Two or three days after this, just about the same time in the afternoon, she was occupied outside in the cook-house when she noticed a queer-looking old woman coming up the avenue to the house. Her strange appearance struck Ann at once as being very peculiar. She said, "Who is it, Father?" Instantly her answer came, "Don't you remember the man who was here the other day?" "Yes, Father, is it him?" "Yes, it is," came the answer.

This time he walked up and said, "I want to see the boss." Although there was not another soul on the farm, Ann said, "Just step in, ma-am, and I will call him." Ann at once ran toward the well, calling at the top of her voice, "Mr. Reid! Mr. Reid!" When the old woman heard her shouting she turned and hobbled away, saying, "Never mind." Ann was sorely tried over this, as it was a question to her mind whether she had not told a lie when she acted in this manner, knowing that Mr. Reid was not around. However, she was somewhat consoled in the remembrance that the first time the man came she had told him the truth, even although her life was in danger.

Another incident occurred years after, when the Reid family had grown up and Ann was living in the little cottage which they had bought for her ere they gave up the old homestead.

When the two girls left home they decided to go out to the far Western States, then just being opened up, and when they left they stored some of their goods in Ann's little cottage. Some of the things were valuable, but they had perfect confidence in Ann's care and integrity. However, it was at this time that a neighbour began to covet possession of these things. The two girls had expected to return home within a year, but instead of that years went by and they were still living in the Western States. The neighbour woman before referred to was one of disreputable character, and while she professed friendship for Ann, yet she did her utmost to undermine her.

On one occasion when Ann was very sick she came in and proffered her services, but Ann had no confidence whatever in the woman, and tried to decline. However, she persistently pressed herself in upon her. Ann suffered greatly from dropsy and heart trouble, and this woman, evidently having designs upon the valuables that she knew were in Ann's care, came in one day and insisted on Ann drinking a cup of tea. Ann had been warned by her Father not to receive anything from her, and when she came in she refused to take it, but the woman fairly glared at Ann and insisted, and under the pressure through fear Ann finally took the cup and drank it. The woman then went out. Ann was sorely tried because she felt she had gone contrary to the revealed will of her Father, and Satan said, "Now He won't hear your prayer." But in an instant Ann was crying out, "Father, forgive me, forgive me. You know I love you better than anything else in the world. But you know I was afraid. Now, Father, like as a father pitieth his children, pity me. You know my frame and you remember that I am but dust."

Instantly she received the assurance of forgiveness, and to her mind was brought at once very vividly the incident in the life of Paul, where he was bitten by the viper, and she received the assurance that God would take care of her, even though poisoned. In a little while she became very, very sick, and vomited incessantly for a long time. She felt that this saved her life. The woman tried to get the care of Ann again, time after time, but by very special providences her efforts along this line were blocked and her purposes frustrated.

Ann firmly believed that in the above instance she had received the fulfilment of the Scripture promise, "If they drink any deadly thing it shall not hurt them."

14

A GODLESS BROTHER

*"I have great sorrow and unceasing pain in my heart
. . . for my brethren's sake, my kinsmen according to
the flesh."*—Romans 9:2, 3.

SOME YEARS AFTER Ann's arrival in this country,
hearing that her only brother was living a very
sinful life, she became concerned about him, and
thinking that he would do better in the New World,
she sent for him. For a while it seemed as though
there was a little change, and he professed to get
converted, but there was no depth to it, and shortly after he plunged more deeply than ever into sin.
He hated to have Ann enter the home, and many
a time in a drunken fit he had threatened her life.
Ann was never afraid of him, however. Once after
she had rebuked him for his sinful life, he picked
up a chair and threatened to kill her with it. Ann
looked at him as bold as a lion, and said, "If the
devil has the chair, my Father has the guiding of
it, and indeed you will not do it." Ann says he
dropped the chair with force enough to have
broken it.

It was a great grief to Ann to see the example

which he set to his little girl. He used to send her
to the saloon for his drink. Ann felt this so keenly
that after rebuking him for it she made it a special
matter of prayer, and getting a glimpse of the life
of sin that seemed inevitable for the little girl under
such surroundings, she cried out to God to save her
and to take her away from the evil which was to
come. She received assurance that this would be
granted, and boldly told her brother that it was
the last time that he would ever be permitted to
send her for his liquor. This enraged him, but did
not alter the decree. For a few days the child
happened to be otherwise occupied when the hour
came to go for the liquor, and then she took sick.
As she grew worse they became very uneasy and
appealed to Ann to pray for the child's recovery.
But she told them plainly that she knew her Father
was going to take the child away to deliver her
from such a wicked home. A few days after this
she fell asleep, leaving behind a clear testimony
of her faith in the Lord Jesus.

Ann did not cease to visit this brother, even
when some miles intervened between them. On
one occasion she was staying with a friend, when
one morning she received word from her Father
that she was to go to see her brother James that

day. Ann replied, "Sure, Father, I cannot go; it is five miles, and I could not walk." The reply came, "You do as I tell you. The earth is the Lord's, and the fulness thereof. The silver and the gold are His, and the cattle upon a thousand hills." Ann saw it in a minute and said, "The horses, too, Father." She went on with her work. Just when she had finished getting dinner ready her Father said, "Now is the time to go." Turning to one of the girls, Ann told her that she must go. They urged her to stay and take her dinner, but Ann insisted that her Father had said, "Now is the time." They said, "Very well, you can do a little errand for us on your way. Just call in and tell Mrs. —— to send over two pounds of butter."

Ann hurried, and away in the distance behind she saw a gray horse coming over the hill. Her Father said, "That is the horse that is to take you." She hurried down the road to get the errand done first. Just before she entered the house she saw the horse stop at the tavern. She at once said, "Sure, Father, that cannot be the one, or it would not stop there." But the answer came, "Yes, that is the horse to take you." When she came out of the house another rig overtook her and she accepted the invitation for a ride, but found the man was only going two miles. After a little while the gray horse overtook them and Ann said to the man who was driving her, "There, that is the horse that my Father said was to take me. Ask the man how far he is going." In reply to this question he said he was just going two miles, but Ann was not satisfied with the answer, and insisted that he ask again. The next time he replied that he was going five miles, and right along the road which Ann desired to go. The man asked him if he would give Ann a ride, as she wanted to go that far. He answered, "I don't take women with me." Ann spoke up then and said, "My Father said that He sent that horse for me." The priest—for such he was—said, "What do you mean? Who is your father?" She replied, "My Heavenly Father." He then said, "Well, jump in."

So Ann got in, and all the way along she talked to the priest about her Father and His wonderful Word. That some impression was made can be judged by the fact that, although the priest was turning off some little way before reaching Ann's destination, he very kindly offered to drive her wherever she wanted to go. Ann thanked him, but got out and walked the rest of the way, praising God for the provision made for her.

She reached the home of her brother, and it seemed as though, while her own brother constantly rejected her message, that God intended her to minister to his wife, for it was not long before this poor woman was wonderfully converted, and the change was just as real and deep as in the life of Ann herself. She was led into an experience of very close intimacy with God, and although living in a drunkard's home she had wonderful answers to her prayers, and led a life that commended the Gospel which she proclaimed.

15

A FAITHFUL SERVANT

"If, therefore, ye have not been faithful in the un-righteous mammon, who will commit to your trust the true riches?"—Luke 16:11.

IT HAS BEEN WRITTEN, "He that is faithful in that which is least shall be made ruler of much," and it is a general principle that those who are untrue in the so-called secular matters of life can never be made powerful in the spiritual realm. Ann kept her covenant with the Reid family, and stayed with them until, first Mrs. Reid, and then later the old doctor, had passed away, nor did her task end then; she continued to keep house for the family that was left until they grew up and her services were required no longer. Even then she constantly followed them with her prayers. Two of the boys left the old homestead and determined to seek their fortunes in the South, and took up residence in New Orleans. A cousin accompanied them on this journey. They had not long resided there when a terrible plague of yellow fever visited the city. People died by hundreds and thousands and were carted away to the outskirts of the city without any ceremony whatever. For two weeks at this period, without knowing what was occurring, Ann had a great burden of prayer, and used to go daily to see her friend, Mrs. Hughes, and together they interceded on behalf of the two absent boys.

During this time Ann had a vision one night that Joshua, the youngest, had died. So certain was she of this that the next morning she visited Mrs. Hughes and told her that she knew Joshua was dead, and that she could no longer pray for him. This friend tried to persuade Ann that it was the constant thought and care for the boys and her undue anxiety that caused her to think thus. But Ann was persistent in stating that her Father had given her the dream, and that it must be so. The cousin kept in correspondence with the two girls who were at home with Ann. He reported that both of the boys had fever, but it was not until six weeks after, when Henry, the other brother, had fully recovered from the fever, that he sent home word that Joshua had died, and when the date became known it was found that it was on the very night of Ann's dream.

When the family needed Ann's services no longer they very kindly fitted up for her a little cottage in the village and made her as comfortable as possible, the boys assuring her that as long as they lived she should never want. However, man's proposals are often very different from that which is brought to pass. It was not long before all the boys were dead and Ann was thrown entirely upon the loving care of her Heavenly Father.

Ann continued to reside in her little cottage for some years, and then for a time returned to the home of a member of the Reid family, but later on accepted an invitation to come and spend a little time with her old friend, Mrs. Hughes, who had moved to the City of Toronto. This temporary arrangement continued for some years, and Toronto became her home. There is no doubt that God's providence was in this, leading Ann into a wider sphere of usefulness and blessing, for her testimony was given in many of the city churches, and her influence was felt far and wide.

16

CORRECTING THE CATHOLIC BISHOP

"Who art thou, that thou art afraid of man that shall die?"—Isaiah 51:12.

SHE WAS NOT POSING as a new Reformer, although even Luther before the Diet of Worms did not stand more fearlessly for the truth than this little Irish woman would when occasion demanded. It is true she was too insignificant a Protestant to cause Rome to tremble, but on the other hand, all the Cardinals and Prelates in the world could not have intimidated this humble saint, or have silenced her tongue when she was moved to speak.

Ann had been detained through stress of weather with a Catholic friend one Saturday night. This good lady pressed her on Sunday morning to accompany her to the Cathedral. In response to the invitation, Ann decided that she would go. The friend took her into one of the front seats, and together they sat while the (to Ann) strange introductory services and ceremonial proceeded. After this came a sermon by the Bishop. Unfortunately, on this occasion his address was taken up with a contrast between Roman Catholicism and the Protestant churches, and he proceeded to take up the various denominations one by one for consideration.

Ann's knowledge of Church history was certainly very limited, and relative claims to antiquity were meaningless to her, as decades, centuries or ages were all alike to her mind. Consequently she understood very little of what was being said until the priest came to the Methodists. Then Ann was all alive at once with interest, as she was now on familiar ground. He commenced by saying that the Methodists were a little, upstart people, founded by a cobbler and in existence but a short time. This was too much for Ann, who immediately stood up and said, "That's not so", and proceeded to explain that they had been in existence for some considerable period, for she had known them for full forty years. Her good friend was mortified and terribly dismayed, and at once tried to pull Ann to her seat. However, Ann was not to be so easily swerved from her position. Turning to her friend, she said, "Stop plucking me; I am not a goose", and proceeded to tell the people what the Methodists were. However, two young priests came toward her, and one of them very respectfully said,

"Madam, it is wrong for you to speak here. The Scriptures say that women much keep silence in the churches, and if they wish to know anything they must ask their husbands at home."

To this remonstrance Ann replied, "I have no husband. I am joined to the Lord, so I will ask Him here", and she at once proceeded to pray. After this she quietly sat in her seat during the rest of the service. The people were so indignant that anyone would dare to contradict their Bishop that they were angry enough to have torn her to pieces at the close, but her friend and some others who knew her came forward and pleaded her cause, and Ann was allowed to go in peace.

Ann was just as bold, however, in her own church. On one occasion they were having a union class meeting at Thornhill, when nearly the whole of the testimonies were simply the confession of heart wanderings and deviations from the will of God, and the whole atmosphere was more like a Jewish wailing place than an old-time Methodist classing meeting. Finally Ann could stand it no longer. She jumped to her feet and marched to the front, and then facing the crowd, she said, "Would to God you'd have done with your heart wanderings and your deviations. You give my

Father's table a bad name. Who, after hearing you this morning, would want to come? You keep people away from the Lord", and then she told them the secret of a joyful Christian life.

17

PRAYER FOR HEALING

*"I have heard thy prayer, I have seen thy tears: behold
I will heal thee."*—2 Kings 20:5.
"The prayer of faith shall save the sick."—James 5:15.

IT IS NOT TO BE wondered at that the remarkable
answers that Ann received to her prayers should
have led people in different distresses to appeal to
Ann for help, and it was not at all an uncommon
thing for the sick to ask for Ann's prayers. There
are many records of wonderful answers along this
line.

While assisting in special services in Brooklyn,
she called on a Mrs. R., who was very low with
typhoid fever. As an aggravating symptom, the
poor patient found it utterly impossible to obtain
sleep. Ann knelt by the bedside in her simple way
and asked her Heavenly Father to give at least
two hours of quiet sleep. As soon as her petition
was ended she went out confidently into the ad-
joining room and asked the members of the family
to keep very quiet, stating that she had asked her
Father to give two hours' sleep, and added, "I
know He will". The patient went right off and

for four hours had quiet, restful sleep, and from that point health began to return.

It must not be thought, however, that Ann would pray indiscriminately according to the requests of the people. She had to learn early that it was impossible to persistently press for answers to prayer that when granted would only prove a hindrance and a curse. On one occasion a husband came to Ann in great distress and said the doctor had given up his wife, and that it was impossible for her to live. Piteously he appealed to Ann to pray for her life to be spared to her family. He said, "I know your faith will bring her back." Ann was entreated and went to her Father in a very presumptuous way and said, "If I am what I profess, I will have her life." She even used stronger expressions which we do not care to repeat. The woman was restored immediately and lived for years a life that dishonoured her Lord and brought discredit on the cause of Christ. Ann humbly confessed the rashness of her prayer.

Some might take exception to the subjects that came within the range of Ann's petitions. I well remember the coming of Ann to our home. After she had been there a short time my youngest brother said to Ann one day, "We haven't seen any of the wonderful things that they tell about done around here since you came." A few days after this one of the cows was taken very sick and Ann heard the men say that she could not get better and must be shot. Ann went out to the pasture field and looked at the cow, and just decided that it was very, very sick, when the Lord said, "Now, here is your chance." Ann said, "Chance for what?" The reply came, "To show them that My power is unchanged." Ann had another look and then decided it was indeed a good chance, but her faith was not staggered by the appearance of things, and she confidently said, "Well, Father, I will take it then by faith," although, Gideon-like, she asked for two or three signs before she was entirely satisfied and could go back and meet my young brother with the assurance that she knew the cow would soon be well. My brother clapped his hands at the statement, and said, "Oh, good! It will get better now." In his boyish way he used to sometimes like to test Ann's faith afterward. When he went back for the cows that night he came home quite disappointed and said, "Ann, it is no better." But this did not disturb Ann's confidence, and shortly after the cow was perfectly restored.

18

THE HABIT OF PRAYER

*"When thou prayest, enter into thy closet, and when
thou hast shut the door, pray to thy Father."*—Matt. 6:6.
*"With all prayer and supplication, praying at all seasons
in the Spirit, and watching thereunto in all
perseverance."*—Eph. 6:18.

WE HAVE REFERRED so often to the manner in
which Ann would go around in constant
conversation and fellowship with God, that some
might be inclined to think that this was the beginning and end of her prayer life. However, she,
from the commencement of the life of victory,
found it absolutely essential to get alone with God,
to enter the closet, to close the door, that she might
pray to her Father in secret. A Salvation Army
officer who had heard Ann testify, and who was
evidently deeply impressed, had a great desire to
know whether her private life was in accord with
her public utterances. Providentially at a special
meeting she was sent for the night to the same
home at which Ann was staying, and they were
put in the same room to sleep.

The officer tells how, long after they had got
into bed, Ann lay quietly communing with her

Father, ejaculating praise from time to time, until nearly midnight. About five o'clock in the morning she awoke, in her usual way, praising God. The dawn had not yet broken, and experiencing some difficulty in finding her clothing, she just asked her Father where the articles were, and at once went to the place, and in her simple way said, "Thank you, Father". Then she poured water into the wash-basin and began to wash. For many years, even to the close of her life, she made it a daily custom to take a complete cold sponge bath. Just as she was preparing for this she suddenly stopped, and addressing God she said, "What is that you say, Father?" Then in a moment she burst out with the exclamation, "Yes, that is it. Thank you, Father." And then with rapture she repeated the following verses: "Then will I sprinkle clean water upon you, and ye shall be clean; from all your filthiness, and from all your idols will I cleanse you. A new heart also will I give you, and a new spirit will I put within you, and I will take away the stony heart out of your flesh, and I will give you an heart of flesh, and I will put My spirit within you and cause you to walk in My statutes, and ye shall keep My judgments and do them." After this she completed her toilet and then knelt in quiet prayer for at least an hour. The officer

104

needed no further demonstration of the secret of Ann's power.

When she came to stay with us, the boys built a little prayer-house for her in the midst of a little grove of cedar trees, near the back of the farm. Every day Ann used to repair for at least two hours to this quiet spot and pour out her soul to God in earnest petition. No one can measure the blessing that came down upon the lives of those for whom she prayed. Frequently she used to take my little brother back with her, and he sometimes served as an incentive to Ann's prayers.

On one occasion Ann asked him where his oldest brother was, and was informed that he had gone with a number of other men to a ploughing-bee to assist one of the neighbours who had been sick all winter, and then closed his remarks by saying, "But it is a pity they will all have to come home", as it was then threatening a regular downpour of rain. Ann expressed her regret at this, and he said, "Why, Ann, couldn't you ask your Father to stop the rain?" and in his boyish way quoted to her her favourite verse, "Faith, mighty faith, the promise sees." Ann at once made this a matter of prayer and received assurance of her answer, and with strong faith asserted that there would be no rainfall that day. The clouds continued to gather and things looked blacker than ever, and George asserted that it was bound to come. But Ann was unmoved, and the men were permitted to finish their day's work without any hindrance from the rain.

Perhaps the writer might be pardoned for referring to a personal experience along the same line. A friend was expected to arrive by train at the depot about five miles from our home. The men were too busy to go, and it had been arranged that I should take the horse and buggy and go to meet him. However, just before the time to leave, a heavy thunder-shower came up. I had always been very much afraid of the lightning, and dreaded the idea of being caught in a thunderstorm away from home. My mother sought to persuade me not to go, as there was no doubt about the storm bursting shortly. We then appealed to Ann, and after quiet communion she turned and said that it was all right for me to go, for not a drop would fall until I had reached my destination. In spite of the gathering storm I drove off, and reached the end of my journey. The horse was put in, and just after meeting my friend the rain began to come down in torrents, and we had a tremendous demonstration of electric power.

19

"OF LIKE PASSIONS WITH US"

"We have this treasure in earthen vessels, that the exceeding greatness of the power may be of God and not from ourselves."—2 Cor. 4:7.

IF WE WERE TO CLOSE this narrative and record an unblemished career of over fifty years, many would think that we were following the custom of hero worshippers, and either with biased judgment or by suppression of facts were creating an ideal rather than recording the actual.

It is with the consciousness that we shall make the lesson of this life more effective thereby, that we venture to insert a few incidents that magnify grace by conclusively proving that the subject of this biography was throughout "a woman of like passions with us".

The Scripture injunction, "Walk in the Spirit", calls for voluntary action, and the exercise of the human will. It is equally possible to "walk after the flesh". Between these two principles, these two "walks", the believer is ever making choice, and to the end of life the will has power to yield to the one or the other. The triumphant Christian life calls for the constant exercise of faith, and union and communion with the Lord. It is written, "He that abideth in Him sinneth not". The whole secret of Ann's victorious life was in this "abiding". While she stayed in the secret place of the Most High there was a wonderful Christlikeness, but immediately her walk of faith ceased there was every manifestation of the old nature apparent.

Mrs. Hughes, with whom Ann lived for many years, narrates two little incidents that illustrate this contrast very vividly. On one occasion Ann was attending a general rally of the Methodists of Toronto, who gathered in the Metropolitan Church for a great love-feast, to be followed by fellowship meeting. Old Dr. Carroll was in the chair. When the opportunity for testimony was given it was not long before Ann was on her feet. The chairman did not know her, and after she had spoken at some length he very courteously reminded her that there were others who were entitled to some time as well as herself. Very sweetly Ann replied, "Yes, that is so; the time is my Father's", and in a very nice way she finished her remarks and sat down.

Before the meeting concluded someone informed Dr. Carroll as to who the old lady was, and he at once felt grieved that he had asked her to stop.

At the conclusion of the service he made his way back to where Ann was standing, and very humbly expressed his regret that he had asked her to cease, and said he hoped she would not be offended. Ann at once said, "Oh, no," and then, lifting up her eyes, she said, "Father, what do you say about it?" At once the answer came and Ann gave it forth from the Scripture, "Great peace have they that love thy law, and nothing shall *offend* them."

In contrast to this, the same friend accompanied Ann to a meeting in Wesley Church, at which, as soon as the opportunity occurred, Ann rose to speak for the Master. As she proceeded, one of the good brethren at the back, evidently impressed and blessed by what she was saying, began to respond. From previous experiences Ann was probably somewhat sensitive, and failing to catch what this good brother said, concluded that he was calling for her to sit down. In a moment she turned around and quite sharply said, "I will not sit down till my Father wants me to." The friend who narrates this said that on her way to the meeting Ann seemed to be just running over with the joy of the Lord, and her face fairly shone as on the street car she spoke to first one and another of the Lord Jesus. Nor had this radiance left her as she rose to speak on this occasion. "But," said this friend, "immediately after her sharp retort there was a change, and after saying a few more things Ann sat down."

On the way home her good friend undertook to remonstrate with her and told her the enemy must have got hold of her ear at least in that meeting. She informed Ann that the person that she had spoken back to was simply saying, "Praise the Lord!" Ann said she thought she heard him say, "Sit down". But on further explanation she became very much ashamed and humbled over her whole attitude in this matter. We simply narrate this here for the purpose of showing that apart from grace and the keeping power of the Holy Spirit, Ann was as liable to be surprised and defeated by the great Adversary as others would be.

There were several occasions on which, during the years that we knew her quite intimately, further evidences of this fact were given. As best illustrating this, we give one little incident that happened toward the close of her life. Ann had been invited by a friend to a city some distance from Toronto, and during her stay in the home of this gentleman, he had become greatly drawn to her, and urged her to spend the remainder of her life in his comfortable home. Through his great kindness Ann had been thrown off her guard and soon became quite infatuated with the peculiar tenets which this man held in regard to the Church as the Bride of Christ. For some three or four years previous Ann had derived great comfort from the truth of the Second Coming of Christ, and looked forward with joy to the time when He should return for His Church, and when all the saints should be "forever with the Lord".

Now, however, she was led off from the plain statements of Scripture, and by degrees the company of those who were to be caught up at the Lord's coming had been restricted and restricted until, standing on the basis practically of human righteousness, there were very few who could be included in the number of those who would rise to meet the Lord in the air at His coming. This friend and Ann were to be amongst the number. So extreme had she become in her view that for the time she seemed to have lost sight of the fundamental basis of grace. Moreover, she became so greatly occupied with this man that she began to apply to him verses of Scripture that could be rightly applied only to the Lord Jesus Himself.

Just at this time my husband was invited to preach in the church to which this gentleman belonged, and was to be entertained at his home. After the sermon Ann rose, and pointing to this man, used the words, "This is my beloved Son; hear ye Him", and directed the people to regard him as one who should be listened to in a peculiar way because of this, and stated that the Church could not be blessed unless they heeded his teaching. She spoke for some time. After the service my husband went home with them, and at the dinner table remarked that he had almost decided to sing Ann down in the meeting when she made such wrong application of Scripture, and demurred at the application of such a verse to any mere man. At this both parties reproved became quite indignant, and Ann gave good evidence of possessing some of the warmth of feeling over which she had wept and prayed so much during her early Christian life. After concluding his Sunday services, my husband decided to leave for home by the early train at five o'clock the next morning.

Just before departing he heard Ann's knock at the door, and on opening it Ann stood outside saying, "My Father tells me that I am to go with you." He was very much surprised at this, as she had told him the day before that she was going to stay in this home the rest of her life. He said to her that

it would be impossible for him to wait while she
got ready, as it was a long walk to the depot, and
he had only just time to hurry on and catch the
train. She insisted, however, that her Father told
her that she was to go with him. He always said
that he wished he had heeded her direction, but he
hurried off to catch the train. After reaching the
depot he had to wait for fully an hour ere the train
came, it was so late that morning.

Little more than a week had elapsed after this
when Ann was sent back to her old home in Toronto under the care of a friend, she having become
utterly irresponsible, and for some months her reason was beclouded and she was under the constant
care of loving friends. Whether her weakening
mental condition was the cause of her deflection
from the truth, or whether a compassionate
Heavenly Father took this method of delivering her
from a subtle delusion, it is impossible to tell. During this period she was in no way responsible for
her actions.

Many friends who had known her for so long
deeply felt her condition, and it was thought it
would be deplorable, after all the years of her testimony, if her life should go out in that manner.
Much prayer was offered up on her behalf, and

after some few months the cloud lifted and she re-gained her wonted mental vigor and spiritual balance, and her remaining years were spent with a clear sky, and declined only, like the orb of day, to a glorious sunset.

20

TESTIMONY OF MINISTERS

"Of honest report, full of the Holy Ghost."—Acts 6:3.
"Obtained a good report through faith."—Heb. 11:39.

THE REV. E. B. RYCKMAN, a Methodist minister, on seeing the obituary notice of Ann's death in one of the papers, wrote as follows to "The Montreal Witness": "Just fifty years ago I was sent to my first station in the Toronto district. My home was at Thornhill, which was also the home of the family of Dr. Reid, in which Ann was a servant, and in a sense mistress and mother, too, for both Dr. and Mrs. Reid had passed away, and the devoted Ann had the young people under her care. I soon discovered that I had in my charge a person and a Christian of very remarkable attainments. During the fifty years of my ministry the word 'consecration' has never been interpreted to me so fully by any other as by Ann. All that is meant by the phrases, 'walking with God' and 'talking with God', was illustrated more visibly, practically and constantly by her than by any other that I have known. One could not talk with her without talking about Christ or some interest of His Kingdom. She was accustomed to speak of the Almighty as was Job, and to hear Him speak to her in turn.

"For instance, one day I went into the Reid home, and of course the subject of religion in some interesting phase of it was up at once between Ann and myself. In the course of conversation, she spoke of her temptations. I said, as if in surprise, 'Why, Ann, how is it that you are tempted?' She replied, 'Oh, I understand it. I told the Lord about it and He said, 'Why, Ann, you are all the time trying to tear down Satan's kingdom, and of course he will not let you alone.' " He then records some incidents already referred to in this narrative and goes on to state: "The most remarkable thing about this woman was her knowledge of Scripture and the use she made of it in prayer, in the relation of Christian experience and in ordinary conversation.

"Generations of Methodist preachers stationed during the past sixty years on Yonge Street circuit have in turn stood astonished at Ann's familiarity with the Bible. All her wants and wishes, her joys and sorrows, indeed, all her thoughts, seemed to be such as could be most easily and fitly expressed in the language of Scripture. I never heard her equal even in the pulpit. Ann made the very highest profession. She affirmed that she was sanctified wholly, and that the blood of Jesus Christ cleansed her from all unrighteousness, and I never knew saint or sinner who knew her that would hint that either her conduct or her character was out of harmony with her profession, and best of all, those who knew her most intimately and the family she served, gave her most readily all credit for sincerity and consistency."

Rev. John Salmon, in writing a few reminiscences of this remarkable life, opens with the statement, "The memory of the just is blessed" (Prov. 10:7). "This was the verse impressed on my mind as I thought of our departed friend and sister in the Lord, Ann Preston, familiarly known by the very suggestive name, 'Holy Ann', or as the Catholics would say, Saint Ann—for she was a saint in the truest sense of that word.

"The memory of her prayer life has often been a benediction to me; so intimate was she with God that when one heard her pray there came a feeling of nearness to the Author of our very being, reminding us of what Moses said when he asked the question, 'What nation is there so great who hath God so nigh unto them as the Lord our God is in all things that we call upon Him for?' (Deut. 4:7). I have often heard Ann, when speaking in

public, quote a passage of Scripture that was
brought to her mind in the following way: The
passage or verse she wanted seemed not to be in
her memory just at the time she wished to give it
out. She would stop and say aloud, 'Father, give
me that verse', and the next instant would exclaim,
'I have got it', and then she would repeat it ver-
batim, so that a person could tell at once that our
sister was living in constant communion with God.

"Like Enoch of old, she walked with God. I
remember on one occasion at a Salvation Army
camp meeting, a number of us were on the platform when Ann was speaking out of the fulness of
her heart. I happened to turn around to my next
neighbour, the (late) honoured and lamented
William Gooderham, and I saw great tears rolling
down his cheeks as that dear woman poured forth
her torrents of living truth from a heart overflowing with love and praise to our God. I cannot at
this time recall her words, but they were words of
wonderful power sent forth by the Holy Spirit
which indwelt that feeble body of clay which was
lighted up by the life Divine so that her face used
to shine with joy and gladness.

"Ann was a genial companion in her home life.
Her conversation usually took the form of her ex-

perience of the Lord's kindness to her under different circumstances. She had no hesitation in saying, 'My Father tells me this', and 'He told me that'. We might be disposed to speak as follows: Something seems to say, do this, or do that. Yes! That Something or Someone. We are afraid to say, 'My Father told me'. Such forms of speech show how little we know of real communion with God. Communion is the highest form of intercourse; it implies that not only do we talk to God, but that He also speaks to us. When the Lord would destroy the cities of the plain, as described in Genesis 18:17-33, He said, "Shall I hide from Abraham that which I do?" Then there begins a conversation between the Lord and Abraham, and after earnest pleading on the part of Abraham that the city should be spared, even if only ten righteous men were found in it, the Lord replied, 'I will not destroy it for the ten's sake'. Then follows the significant statement, 'And the Lord went his way as soon as he had left communing with Abraham, and Abraham returned to his place'. Communion consisted thus in the Lord talking to Abraham and Abraham talking to God.

"Our beloved sister Ann knew what it was thus to hold converse. Is that not what is meant when the Lord Jesus says, 'My sheep hear my voice and I know them, and they follow me?' Ours is the privilege to speak to the Master and to have the Master speak to us. Solomon prayed for a hearing heart (marginal reading), a heart to hear God's voice.

"On one occasion I was taking our sister Ann to spend a few weeks in a home near Whitby. During the passage on the train there sat behind us a Catholic priest, who became very much interested in the conversation going on between Ann and myself. I drew her out in regard to the dealings of the Lord with her in answer to prayer. By and by the priest put several questions to her, which were usually answered in Scripture language. He looked at her with wonder and certain amount of admiration, as much as to say, 'Here is an uneducated old Irishwoman who evidently knows more about vital godliness than I do. What does it all mean?' He was evidently much impressed with her conversation, and who can tell what the result might be?"

Ann was always ready, in season and out of season, to give a reason for the hope that was in her. On the street car or train, in the home or on the street, she was quick to grasp the opportunity, without fear, to speak for her Lord.

Pastor Salmon continues as follows: "On one occasion Dr. Zimmerman and I were out making pastoral calls, when we went into a house and learned that our sister Ann was very sick in bed. We were ushered into a room and found she had been praying to God to send us to see her. As we waited upon God in prayer, Ann poured out her heart something like this: 'Father, sure the devil told me that my two brothers would not come to see me, as they did not know I was sick, and that I could not write to tell them how ill I was. But, Father, you told me I could telegraph them by way of the Throne of Grace. So I just telegraphed to you, and now you have sent the message to them, and here they are. Glory to God!' We were filled with holy joy and laughter, and could do nothing but praise God from the bottom of our hearts. God graciously answered prayer, and Ann was immediately restored to health, and testified afterward to having been raised up from a sick bed in answer to the prayer of faith given to us on that memorable visit."

We could give the testimony of many other ministers, did space permit. At her funeral almost every evangelical denomination was represented, and minister after minister rose to bear witness to the wonderful influence of the life that had just closed. Ann did not hesitate to exhort, rebuke or reprove ministers when she felt they were not true to the Word of God or to the light given to them, and more than one was led to greater faithfulness in their ministry through the faithful testimony of this humble saint.

The well-known Bible teacher, Mr. W. R. Newell, gives the following testimony concerning the way in which Ann would obtain knowledge concerning individual lives in communion with her Heavenly Father. He writes:

"Several winters ago I was holding meetings in Toronto, and was staying with my wife at the China Inland Mission Home.

"One day I suggested we go to visit 'Holy Ann', whom I had met, and with whose life and testimony I was profoundly impressed.

"We had an excellent talk with her. She seemed on fire with the Word of God, being occupied with nothing else. She would bring up passage after passage with a kind of holy triumph that was most refreshing.

"In the midst of her conversation she suddenly turned to my wife and said, 'Many are the afflictions of the righteous, but the Lord delivereth them out of them all. I think you will be sick. There will some trouble come to you, I think, pretty soon, but the Lord will deliver you out of it.' She said this with much earnestness and conviction, as if she had Divine light on the subject.

"My wife and I spoke of the matter as we walked back to the Mission. On the next day, or the next day but one, my wife became ill with pneumonia of an acute type, and came very near the gates of the grave, being very low for several weeks, but she recovered, just as had been said by this remarkable handmaiden of the Lord.

"I was never in my life so impressed with what seemed to be prophetic insight, as on this occasion."

21

SUNSET

"I heard a voice from heaven saying, Write, Blessed are the dead which die in the Lord from henceforth: yea, saith the Spirit, that they may rest from their labours: for their works do follow them."—Rev. 14:13.

IN HER EARLY Christian life Ann had been taught to look upon death as the culminating point in Christian experience, ushering into all that was perfect. She had experienced the taking away of the sting of death, and one of her favourite utterances in her testimony was that "sudden death" to her would be "sudden glory". However, in her later life she had from the Scriptures been taught to look for the personal return of the Lord Jesus, and it was to her a bright hope of the future. However, as the days and years flew by she sometimes became a little weary, and on several occasions again expressed her willingness, and even desire, to depart and be with the Lord. The last few months of life, however, were full of great activity and constant witnessing.

The Sunday before she passed away she was up as usual and present at the seven o'clock prayer meeting in the Berkeley Street Methodist Church. After her breakfast she went again to the class meeting and stayed for the preaching service. When the benediction was pronounced, she, with others, went up to say goodbye to the minister, Rev. Marmaduke Pearson, who was leaving for another charge. In her conversation with him she had not noticed that she had got up on the low platform, and gradually moving back, she stepped over the edge and fell with considerable force to the floor. However, she rose and did not seem to feel very much the worse for the little accident, and in the afternoon went out again to attend another meeting. Other than being somewhat wearied, there seemed to be no change when she retired to rest that evening, and she rose up as usual on Monday morning, took her customary bath, but just as she sat down to breakfast she was smitten with a stroke of paralysis. She gradually sank into semi-consciousness. Mrs. Pedlow, the humble widow who had gladly shared her home with Ann during the last years of her life, was away at the time. She was immediately summoned home. During the intervening hours Ann lay with eyes wide open, but observing Mrs. Pedlow's arrival she seemed to be satisfied, and the weary eyelids closed. For three days she lay perfectly still, and yet seemed to understand what was going on, for when asked to press the hand if she understood what was being said, or if she knew who was speaking, she would at once respond with gentle pressure.

After lingering for a few days, she quietly slept away on Thursday, June 21st, 1906, at the age of 96. The sun was sinking in the west on the longest day of the year. Mrs. Pedlow and a few friends were watching by the couch. As the vital flame burned low, they sang softly:

"Abide with me, fast falls the eventide,
The darkness deepens: Lord with me abide;
When other helpers fail, and comforts flee,
Help of the helpless, O abide with me."

Just as the words, "Swift to its close ebbs out life's little day", broke the stillness of the room, the spirit quietly took its flight and the dear old saint was present with the Lord she loved. As soon as it was known, the home was thronged by hundreds anxious to get a last glimpse of the loved face, and on Saturday a fitting tribute was paid, when, in the Berkeley Street Methodist Church, the friends gathered to take part in the last service.

The church was packed with friends, some of whom had come many miles to be present at that service. Ministers of six different denominations who had known her life paid fitting tribute in their testimony on this occasion to its influence and power in the lives of others. At the close of the service many followed to the cemetery at Mount Pleasant, where the body was interred. The earthly life has ended, but its influence is still felt. Although her voice is no longer heard, this tribute to her memory is inscribed that the record of her words and deeds may continue to bring glory to the Father, with Whom she lived in such intimate fellowship; to the Son, through the merit of whose blood alone she claimed redemption; to the Holy Spirit, by Whose power she was quickened and kept; to the abounding grace of God, through which alone she was on earth what she now is in heaven,

"HOLY ANN."